Practice Book

CENTER STAGE

2

Express Yourself in English

Lynn Bonesteel
Samuela Eckstut-Didier

Series Consultants

MaryAnn Florez   **Sharon Seymour**

PEARSON
Longman

Center Stage 2: Express Yourself in English
Practice Book

Pearson Education, 10 Bank Street, White Plains, NY 10606

Staff credits: The people who made up the **Center Stage 2 Practice Book** team,
representing editorial, production, design, and manufacturing are
Pietro Alongi, Wendy Campbell, Diane Cipollone, Dave Dickey,
Warren Fischbach, Aliza Greenblatt, Ray Keating, and Melissa Leyva.

Text composition: ElectraGraphics, Inc.

Text font: 9.5/11 Minion Pro

Photo credits: p. 1 (first) LWA-Dann Tardif/zefa/Corbis, (second) Royalty-free/Corbis,
(third) Leland Bobbe/Corbis; **p. 2** Medio Images/Getty Images;
p. 3 (first) Michael Prince/Corbis, (second) LWA-Dann Tardif/zefa/Corbis;
p. 30 Chris Trotman/New Sport/Corbis; **p. 72** Royalty-free/Corbis

Illustration credits: A Corazón Abierto (Marcela Gómez), Steve Attoe,
Kenneth Batelman, Keith Batcheller, Precision Graphics, Marty Harris,
Alan King, Luis Montiel, Francisco Morales, Mari Rodríguez,
Roberto Sadí, John Schreiner, Gary Torrisi, Cam Wilson

ISBN-13: 978-0-13-607017-7
ISBN-10: 0-13-607017-5

Pearsonlongman on the Web
Pearsonlongman.com offers online resources for teachers and students.
Access our Companion Websites, our online catalog, and our local offices around the world.
Visit us at **pearsonlongman.com.**

Printed in the United States of America

1 2 3 4 5 6 7 8 9 10—BR—12 11 10 09 08

Contents

NAME: _____   DATE: _____

UNIT 1 VOCABULARY EXERCISES

 A   **Look at the pictures. Complete the sentences. Use the words in the boxes.**

middle-aged	old	~~young~~

8   45   70

1. She is ___young___.   **2.** He is _____.   **3.** They are _____.

average weight	heavy	thin

Tom   Ann   Lee

4. Ann is _____.   **5.** Tom is _____.   **6.** Lee is _____.

beautiful	good-looking

7. He is _____. **8.** She is _____.

average height	short	tall

9. The men are _____.

10. The women are _____.

11. The people are not _____.

B Read the conversation. Then complete the sentences. Use the words in the box.

Olga: Hello, I'm Olga. I'm from Colombia. It's nice to meet you. Are you in this class, too? The teacher is good-looking! And he's young, too! Is he married? Ha ha!

Eiko: Hi. I'm Eiko.

~~funny~~	quiet	serious	talkative

1. Olga is _____funny_____ and _____.

2. Eiko is _____ and _____.

NAME: _____ DATE: _____

UNIT 1 GRAMMAR EXERCISES

Grammar to Communicate 1:
Be: Affirmative and Negative Statements

 A   Complete the sentences. Use *am*, *is*, or *are*.

Hi! I _____am_____ Lisa.
    1.
I _____ 20 years old.
      2.

Lisa _____ young. She _____ not old.
         3.   4.

Hi! I _____ Becky. I _____ 8.
       5.   6.
    Lisa and I _____ not old.
                  7.
    We _____ young.
          8.

B   Complete the sentences. Use *am*, *is*, or *are* in the first sentence. Use a contraction and *not* in the second sentence.

1. David _____is_____ young. He_'s not_____ old.

2. Makiko_____ short. She _____ tall.

3. I _____ middle-aged. I _____ young.

4. André and Michele _____ funny. They _____ serious.

5. Tina and I _____ single. We _____ married.

6. You and Rosario _____ average height. You _____ short.

Grammar to Communicate 2:
Be: Yes / No Questions and Short Answers

A **Match the questions with the answers. Write the correct letters.**

_c_ **1.** Is Lara a student?	**a.** Yes, he is.
_____ **2.** Is Bob a teacher?	**b.** Yes, I am.
_____ **3.** Are the students friendly?	**c.** ~~Yes, she is.~~
_____ **4.** Are you a good student?	**d.** Yes, we are.
_____ **5.** Is this Unit 1?	**e.** Yes, they are.
_____ **6.** Are we on page 2?	**f.** Yes, it is.

B **Write questions about you and people you know. Put the words in the correct order. Then answer the questions. Use short answers.**

1. A: _____ Is your class noisy? _____
       (your class / noisy / is)

   B: _____ Yes, it is. OR No, it's not. _____

2. A: _____
       (you / are / married)

   B: _____

3. A: _____
       (your classmates / talkative / are)

   B: _____

4. A: _____
       (average height / you / are)

   B: _____

5. A: _____
       (funny / is / your best friend)

   B: _____

6. A: _____
       (your teacher / is / tall)

   B: _____

Grammar to Communicate 3:
Regular Count Nouns and Irregular Nouns

 A Look at the pictures. Complete the sentences about the people. Write singular or plural nouns.

A

B

1. Two _____ men _____ are in Picture A.
        (man)

2. Two _____ are in Picture A.
        (woman)

3. Three _____ are in Picture B.
        (child)

4. One _____ is a girl.
        (child)

5. Two children are _____.
                        (boy)

6. Seven _____ are in the two _____.
            (person)   (picture)

B Rewrite the sentences. Make the nouns plural.

1. The person is hardworking.   _____ The people are hardworking. _____

2. The man is tall.   _____

3. The girl is smart.   _____

4. The child is noisy.   _____

5. The teacher is friendly.   _____

6. The woman is funny.   _____

7. The boy is good-looking.   _____

8. The class is small.   _____

Review and Challenge

Correct the conversation. There are ten mistakes. The first mistake is corrected for you.

Yuri: ~~You~~ *Are you* a new student?

Vu: Yes, I'am. My name is Vu.

Yuri: Hi. I'm Yuri. This class good.

Vu: Is it big?

Yuri: No, it not. Is small—six mans and seven woman.

Vu: Are the students nice?

Yuri: Yes, they are. The studentes are friendly.

Vu: Is nice the teacher?

Yuri: Yes, she is. She no is strict.

UNIT 2 VOCABULARY EXERCISE

Look at the family tree. Complete the sentences with family words. Use the words in the boxes.

aunt	daughter	mother	~~sister~~	uncle
~~brother~~	father	nephew	son	wife
~~cousins~~	husband	niece		

1. Jenny and Ted are ___*sister*___ and ___*brother*___ .

2. Tina and Joan are _____ and _____ .

3. Roger and Ted are _____ and _____ .

4. Linda and Burt are _____ and _____ .

5. Arthur and Jenny are _____ and _____ .

6. Shelly and Mike are _____ and _____ .

7. Ted, Jenny, Mike, and Tina are _____ .

brother-in-law	grandfather	grandparents	parents
father-in-law	grandmother	mother-in-law	sister-in-law

8. Roger and Joan are _____ and _____.

9. Linda and Burt are the _____ of Ted, Jenny, Mike, and Tina.

10. Joan and Arthur are the _____ of Ted and Jenny.

11. Burt is the _____ of Mike and Tina.

12. Linda is the _____ of Jenny and Ted.

13. Burt is the _____ of Joan and Shelly.

14. Linda is the _____ of Joan and Shelly.

UNIT 2 GRAMMAR EXERCISES

Grammar to Communicate 1:
Possessive Adjectives

A   **Complete the story. Use *my, your, his, our,* or *their*.**

Hi! ____My____ name is Tina. I'm 14, and _____ brother
          1.   2.
is 15. _____ name is Mike. _____ parents are 40.
          3.   4.
_____ names are Shelly and Roger. How about you? Tell
    5.
me about _____ family!
            6.

B   **Look at Antonio's family tree. Then complete the sentences with possessive adjectives and family words. Use capital letters if necessary.**

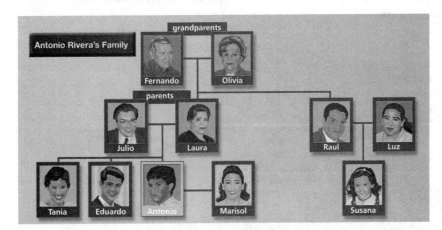

1. Antonio is 25. Marisol is ____his____ ____wife____. Julio
    and Laura are _____ _____. Olivia and
    Fernando are _____ _____.

2. Susana is 4. Antonio is _____ _____.
    Luz is _____ _____. Julio is _____ _____.

3. Laura is 50. Raul is _____ _____.
    Eduardo is _____ _____, and
    Susana is _____ _____.

4. Eduardo is 28, and Tania is 23. Marisol is _____ _____.
    Fernando is _____ _____.

NAME: _____   DATE: _____

Grammar to Communicate 2:
Possessive Nouns

 A **Complete the sentences. Circle the correct words.**

1. Her **aunt's / aunts'** names are Linda and Mabel.

2. My **brothers / brother's** dog is big.

3. Uncle Matt's **wife's / wife** is tall.

4. **Henry and June's / Henry's and June's** sons are middle-aged.

5. The **children's / childrens'** school is good.

6. Their **parents' / parent's** friends are from Chile.

7. His **brother's-in-law's / brother-in-law's** house is small.

B **Look again at Antonio's family tree. Complete the sentences with possessive nouns.**

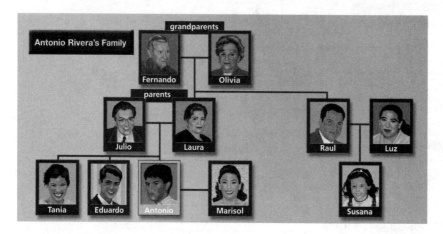

1. _____Antonio's_____ wife is Marisol.

2. _____ mother is Luz.

3. _____ children are Raul and Laura.

4. _____ brothers are Eduardo and Antonio.

5. _____ niece is Susana.

6. _____ sister-in-law is Tania.

Grammar to Communicate 3:
Be: Information questions

A   Match the questions with the answers. Write the correct letters.

   _d_   **1.** How are you?　　　　　　**a.** At school.

  _____   **2.** Where are they?　　　　　**b.** At 4:00 P.M.

  _____   **3.** What is it?　　　　　　　**c.** Six feet.

  _____   **4.** How tall is he?　　　　　**d.** ~~Fine, thanks.~~

  _____   **5.** When is the movie?　　　　**e.** Twenty.

  _____   **6.** Who are they?　　　　　　**f.** France.

  _____   **7.** How old are you?　　　　　**g.** A cat.

  _____   **8.** Where is she from?　　　　**h.** My cousins.

B   Read the answers. Then write questions.

1. A: _What is Makiko's last name?_____

    B: Makiko's last name is Kakutani.

2. A: _____

    B: Ned is 30 years old.

3. A: _____

    B: Liliana is 5 feet 3 inches.

4. A: _____

    B: Polly's telephone number is 555-2335.

5. A: _____

    B. Charlie's English class is at 4:00 P.M.

6. A: _____

    B: My husband's sister is in the picture.

7. A: _____

    B: My parents are in New York City.

NAME: _____   DATE: _____

Review and Challenge

Find the mistake in each conversation. Circle the letter and correct the mistake.

1. **A:** <u>What</u> is Tracy <u>from</u>?   **Correct:** _Where is Tracy from?_
        (A)   B

    B: Tracy <u>is</u> <u>from</u> Texas.
            C   D

2. **A:** <u>How old</u> is <u>your</u> <u>fathers</u> friend?   **Correct:** _____
            A   B   C

    B: He <u>is</u> 55 years old.
            D

3. **A:** <u>What</u> are her <u>daughters'</u> names?   **Correct:** _____
            A   B

    B: <u>Their</u> names <u>is</u> Lisa and Anita.
            C   D

4. **A:** <u>How tall</u> is your <u>cousin's</u> husband?   **Correct:** _____
            A   B

    B: <u>Your</u> cousin's husband <u>is</u> 6 feet 3 inches.
            C   D

5. **A:** <u>How</u> are your <u>sister's</u> <u>sons</u>?   **Correct:** _____
            A   B   C

    B: <u>Their</u> fine.
            D

6. **A:** <u>Who</u> is your <u>aunt's</u> telephone number?   **Correct:** _____
            A   B

    B: <u>My</u> <u>aunt's</u> telephone number is 444-2222.
            C   D

7. **A:** <u>Where</u> is <u>Betty's</u> and <u>Linda's</u> house?   **Correct:** _____
            A   B   C

    B: <u>It's</u> in Brentwood.
            D

8. **A:** <u>When</u> is <u>your</u> <u>mothers'</u> English class?   **Correct:** _____
            A   B   C

    B: <u>It's</u> at 10:00 A.M.
            D

9. **A:** <u>Where</u> is <u>your</u> <u>childrens'</u> school?   **Correct:** _____
            A   B   C

    B: <u>Their</u> school is across the street.
            D

UNIT 3 VOCABULARY EXERCISE

Look at the pictures. What are the people's jobs? Write sentences. Use the words in the box.

John Yu
1

Lili Sanchez
2

Ali Rashid
3

Mónica Gómez
4

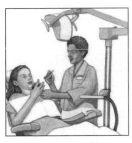

Lynn Goulet
5

Michael Johnson
6

Marina Petrov
7

Pete Murphy
8

Meg Sullivan
9

She says, "I don't understand."

Tôi Không muon.

Nicole Byrns
10

Julio Dandelet
11

Mario Tecce
12

Maria Recine
13

an accountant	a dentist	a hairdresser	a nurse	a waiter
an attorney	an electrician	an interpreter	a plumber	a waitress
a cook	an engineer	a mechanic		

1. He is an accountant.
2. _____
3. _____
4. _____
5. _____
6. _____
7. _____
8. _____
9. _____
10. _____
11. _____
12. _____
13. _____

UNIT 3 GRAMMAR EXERCISES

Grammar to Communicate 1:
A and *An*

A **Complete each sentence. Circle the correct answer and write it on the line.**

1. Peter is _____*a waiter*_____.
    (waiter / (a waiter))

2. Tomas is _____.
    (dentist / a dentist)

3. Nicole is _____.
    (a hairdresser / an hairdresser)

4. Abdulkarim is _____.
    (a interpreter / an interpreter)

5. Nadia and Vikram are _____.
    (attorneys / an attorneys)

6. Nancy and Ruth are _____.
    (nurses / a nurses)

B **Read the charts. Then write sentences about the people's jobs.**

	NAME	JOB
1	Jack	cook
2	Carmen	hairdresser
3	Marisol	interpreter
4	Mohammed	mechanic

	NAME	JOB
5	Bao	engineer
6	Esteban	doctor
7	Lucy	engineer
8	Mike	mechanic

1. Jack _____*is a cook.*_____

2. Carmen _____

3. Marisol _____

4. Mohammed _____

5. Bao _____

6. Esteban _____

7. Lucy and Bao _____

8. Mike and Mohammed _____

Grammar to Communicate 2:
Adjectives and Noun Word Order

 Circle the adjectives in the sentences.

Meg is a (good) hairdresser. She is careful. She is a fast worker. She isn't messy. Meg's job is interesting. Her boss is a nice woman. Meg is happy at her job.

B Complete each sentence. Circle the correct answer.

1. Luis is a _____.
   a. worker fast   b. fast worker

2. Anna's job is _____.
   a. boring   b. a boring

3. A _____ is patient.
   a. teacher good   b. good teacher

4. My classmates are _____.
   a. kinds   b. kind

5. My new job is _____.
   a. interesting job   b. an interesting job

6. _____ are honest and careful.
   a. Good accountants   b. Goods accountants

7. Aden is _____ at his job.
   a. good   b. a good

8. Bella is _____ attorney.
   a. a honest   b. an honest

Grammar to Communicate 3:
A / An / Ø and *The*

A   Look at the picture. For each sentence, write *T* (true) or *F* (false).

Yoko   Lisa   Veronica   Alice

___T___ **1.** Alice is a cook.

_____ **2.** Lisa is a cook.

_____ **3.** The short woman is Yoko.

_____ **4.** The tall woman is Lisa.

_____ **5.** Yoko and Lisa are the waitresses.

_____ **6.** Veronica and Alice are the cooks.

B Complete the conversations. Write *a*, *Ø*, or *the*.

1. Carlos: Liz, what do you do?

    Liz: I'm __*a*__ nurse.

2. Bob: What is Danny's job?

    Jim: He is _____ mechanic.

3. Dave: Henry, what do you and Ali do?

    Henry: We're _____ cooks.

4. Liz: Who is the little boy in _____ picture?

    Carlos: My son.

5. Tim: Who is he?

    Stan: Mr. Sullivan. He's _____ boss.

    Tim: Is he _____ good boss?

    Stan: Yeah, he's _____ nice.

6. Mona: Are you _____ new student?

    Julia: Yes, I am. I'm Julia.

    Mona: Hi. I'm Mona. I'm _____ new, too.

    Julia: Who is _____ tall woman? Is she the teacher?

    Mona: Yes, she is.

Review and Challenge

Complete the conversations. Use the words in the box.

~~a~~	engineer	mechanic	nurses
an	interesting	messy	the

1. **A:** What do you do?

   B: I'm _____ a _____ waiter.

2. **A:** Is Chuck a teacher?

   B: No. He's _____ accountant.

3. **A:** What is Osman's job?

   B: He's a _____.

4. **A:** What does Tatiana do?

   B: She's an _____.

5. **A:** Are Nancy and Monica doctors?

   B: No. They're _____.

6. **A:** Are you happy at your job?

   B: Yes, I am. My job is _____.

7. **A:** Who is _____ boy in the picture?

   B: He's my son.

8. **A:** Is Ashley's apartment neat?

   B: No. It's _____.

UNIT 4 VOCABULARY EXERCISE

Complete the sentences. Use the words in the boxes.

airport	hospital	~~museum~~	shopping mall
apartment building	movie theater	restaurant	supermarket

1. The *Mona Lisa* is in a _____ *museum* _____.

2. Stores are in a _____.

3. Cooks are in a _____.

4. Nurses are in a _____.

5. Mechanics are at an _____.

6. Food is in a _____.

7. The people are at home. They're in a tall _____.

8. A funny movie is at the _____.

buildings	café	hotel	office building	outdoor market	stores

9. The Empire State Building is an _____. It is a nice workplace.

10. Waitresses are in a _____.

11. Tokyo is a big city. Many _____ are in Tokyo.

12. The _____ is in the park. The food is not expensive.

13. Kmart, H&M, and Target are _____.

14. The Hilton is an expensive _____.

NAME: _____   DATE: _____

UNIT 4 GRAMMAR EXERCISES

Grammar to Communicate 1:
There is / There are: Statements

 A Complete the sentences about River City. Use *There is* or *There are.*

1. _____There are_____ two supermarkets on River Street.

2. _____ a movie theater across from Super Food.

3. _____ a shopping mall next to the theater.

4. _____ two restaurants on the street, too.

5. _____ a park on Center Street.

6. _____ trees in the park.

B Look at the map of River City. Complete the sentences with *is, isn't, are,* or *aren't.*

1. There _____isn't_____ a park on River Street.

2. There _____ a hospital on Center Street.

3. There _____ supermarkets on River Street.

4. There _____ supermarkets on Elm Street.

5. There _____ a movie theater on Center Street.

6. There _____ a movie theater on River Street.

Grammar to Communicate 2:
Some / A lot of / Any

A **Complete the sentences. Use *some* or *any*.**

1. There are _____some_____ tall buildings in my hometown.

2. There are _____ nice stores on Main Street.

3. There aren't _____ hairdressers on Main Street.

4. There aren't _____ big banks.

5. There are _____ trees in the parks.

6. There aren't _____ buildings in the parks.

B **Look at the map of River City on page 1. Complete the sentences. Use *is*, *isn't*, *are*, or *aren't*.**

1. There _____are_____ a lot of buildings in River City.

2. There _____ some stores in the picture.

3. There _____ any taxi cabs on the streets.

4. There _____ a hotel next to the movie theater.

5. There _____ some students on Elm Street.

6. There _____ a lot of people in the park.

7. There _____ any museums in River City.

8. There _____ an airport in the picture.

Grammar to Communicate 3:
Is there / Are there

A Complete each conversation. Circle the correct answer and write it on the line.

1. A: _____Is there_____ a desert in your country?
        (Is there / There is)

    B: Yes, _____.
              (there is / there's)

2. A: _____ any mountains?
              (Are there / There are)

    B: No, _____.
              (they aren't / there aren't)

3. A: Are there _____ tall buildings in your country?
                        (a / any)

    B: Yes, there are _____ lot of tall buildings.
                              (a / some)

        _____ are in my city.
              (There / They)

4. A: Is there a famous museum in your city?

    B: Yes, there is. _____ is next to the river.
                              (There / It)

B Complete the questions with *Is there* or *Are there*. Use *a, an,* or *any*.

1. ___Are there any tall buildings___ in your hometown?
              (tall buildings)

2. _____ in your hometown?
              (river)

3. _____ in your hometown?
              (nice restaurants)

4. _____ in your hometown?
              (old college)

5. _____ in your hometown?
              (good hospitals)

6. _____ in your hometown?
              (lake)

Review and Challenge

Find the mistake in each conversation. Circle the letter and correct the mistake.

1. **A:** <u>Is there</u> <u>an</u> art museum here?
         A   B

    B: Yes, there <u>are</u>. It's on Park Avenue.
             Ⓒ

    Correct: _Yes, there is._

2. **A:** <u>There is</u> a new bank on Center Street.
         A

    B: There <u>are</u> a new bank <u>on Maple Street</u>, too.
           B   C

    Correct: _____

3. **A:** <u>Are there</u> cheap apartments in your hometown?
         A

    B: No, there <u>are</u>. The apartments <u>are</u> expensive.
            B   C

    Correct: _____

4. **A:** <u>There is</u> <u>a good restaurant</u> next to the movie theater.
         A   B

    B: <u>There's</u> good restaurants on Water Street, too.
         C

    Correct: _____

5. **A:** <u>There are</u> <u>a lot of store</u> here.
         A   B

    B: Yes, there are. <u>They're</u> good stores.
                C

    Correct: _____

6. **A:** <u>Is there</u> a mall <u>across from</u> the hospital?
         A   B

    B: No, there aren't <u>some</u> stores on Green Street.
              C

    Correct: _____

7. **A:** <u>Is there</u> a famous waterfall <u>in your country</u>?
         A   B

    B: No, <u>it</u> isn't.
          C

    Correct: _____

8. **A:** <u>Is</u> there <u>any</u> good schools here?
         A   B

    B: Yes, <u>there are</u>.
           C

    Correct: _____

UNIT 5 VOCABULARY EXERCISES

A   **Read the sentences. Write the name of the food or drink. Use the words in the box.**

apples	carrots	fruit	milk	spinach	~~tomatoes~~
bananas	cookies	juice	oranges	tea	vegetables
candy	eggs	meat	soup		

1. They're red. They're _____ tomatoes _____.

2. They're yellow fruit. They're _____.

3. They're red or green fruit. They're _____.

4. It's a green vegetable. It's _____.

5. They're orange fruit. They're _____.

6. They're orange vegetables. They're _____.

7. It's a white drink. It's in a carton. It's _____.

8. It's a fruit drink. It's in a carton. It's _____.

9. It's a hot drink. It's in a box. It's _____.

10. It's in a can. It's _____.

11. It's in a bag. It's sweet. It's _____.

12. They're in a package. They're sweet. They're _____.

13. They're white. They're from a chicken. They're _____.

14. Apples and bananas are _____.

15. Carrots and spinach are _____.

16. Beef and chicken are _____.

B Look at the pictures. Write the names of the foods. Use the words in the box.

a box of rice	bread	fish	mayonnaise
beef	chicken	ice cream	

1. _____bread_____   5. _____

2. _____   6. _____

3. _____   7. _____

4. _____

UNIT 5 GRAMMAR EXERCISES

Grammar to Communicate 1:
Count and Noncount Nouns

A Complete the questions. Use *is* or *are*.

1. How much ____are____ the apples?   They're $1.49 a pound.

2. How much _____ the milk?   It's $2.19.

3. How much _____ the eggs?   They're $2.09.

4. How much _____ the bread?   It's $3.39.

5. How much _____ the chicken?   It's $4.19 a pound.

6. How much _____ the candy?   It's 75¢.

7. How much _____ the tomatoes?   They're $2.99 a pound.

B Complete the sentences about prices in your country. Use *is, isn't, are,* or *aren't*.

1. Vegetables _are OR aren't_ expensive.

2. Beef _____ expensive.

3. Oranges _____ expensive.

4. Fresh fish _____ expensive.

5. Carrots _____ expensive.

6. Rice _____ expensive.

7. Soup _____ expensive.

8. Bananas _____ expensive.

Grammar to Communicate 2:
Quantifiers: *Some / A little / A lot of / A few / Any*

A   **Complete the sentences. Use *a little* or *a few*.**

1. There is ___*a little*___ butter on the bread.

2. There are _____ nuts in the cookies.

3. There is _____ sugar in the tea.

4. There is _____ cheese in the sandwiches.

5. There are _____ cookies on the counter.

6. There are _____ peppers on the pizza.

B   **Read the recipe. Complete the conversation. Circle the correct answer and write it on the line.**

Ann: The soup _____*is*_____ good. What's in it?
                1. (is / are)

Jess: Well, there are _____ tomatoes, and there _____
                      2. (a little / a lot of)   3. (is / are)

   a lot of spinach. There is _____ water, and there
                                         4. (some / any)

   _____ two onions.
      5. (is / are)

Ann: What about milk?

Jess: No, there isn't _____ milk.
                             6. (some / any)

Ann: Salt and pepper?

Jess: Yes, there is _____ salt and _____ of pepper.
                          7. (a little / a few)   8. (a little / a lot)

   There is _____ butter, too.
                9. (some / a few)

Grammar to Communicate 3:
Count and Noncount Nouns: Questions

A   **Look at the picture. Answer the questions.**

1.   Are there any tomatoes on the table?   _No, there aren't._

2.   Is there any fruit on the table?   _____

3.   Are there any eggs on the table?   _____

4.   Is there any salt on the table?   _____

5.   Is there any pepper on the table?   _____

6.   Are there any peppers on the table?   _____

B   **Write questions. Use *How much* or *How many*.**

1.   **A:**   (soda) _____ How much soda is there? _____

     B: There are six cans.

2.   **A:**   (rice) _____

     B: There are two bags.

3.   **A:**   (cookies) _____

     B: There's one box.

4.   **A:**   (juice) _____

     B: Two bottles.

5.   **A:**   (carrots) _____

     B: One bag.

6.   **A:**   (eggs) _____

     B: There are two cartons of eggs.

NAME: _____   DATE: _____

Review and Challenge

Find the mistake in each conversation. Circle the letter and correct the mistake.

1. **A:** <u>The beef</u> <u>are</u> $8.99 <u>a pound</u>.
        A   (B)   C

   B: It's expensive!

   Correct: _The beef is $8.99 a pound._

2. **A:** Where's <u>the</u> <u>fruit</u>?
             A B

   B: <u>They're</u> on the table.
       C

   Correct: _____

3. **A:** <u>How much</u> potatoes <u>are there</u>?
         A   B

   B: <u>There's</u> one bag of potatoes.
       C

   Correct: _____

4. **A:** <u>How much</u> <u>are</u> <u>the candy</u>?
         A   B   C

   B: It's 99¢.

   Correct: _____

5. **A:** Are there <u>any bananas</u>?
                A

   B: There <u>are</u> <u>a little</u> bananas.
         B   C

   Correct: _____

6. **A:** <u>How many</u> soda is there?
        A

   B: <u>There are</u> four <u>cans</u>.
       B   C

   Correct: _____

7. **A:** <u>Is there</u> <u>any coffee</u>?
       A   B

   B: <u>Yes, there's</u>. It's in Aisle 4.
       C

   Correct: _____

8. **A:** <u>Is there</u> <u>any salt</u> in the soup?
       A   B

   B: There's <u>a few</u> salt.
          C

   Correct: _____

9. **A:** <u>Is there</u> <u>any cookies</u> <u>in the box</u>?
       A   B   C

   B: There's one.

   Correct: _____

NAME: _____   DATE: _____

UNIT 6 VOCABULARY EXERCISES

A Look at the pictures. Write the activities. Use the words in the box.

do exercises	play soccer	ride a bike	swim
go for a walk	play tennis	~~run~~	

1. _____ run _____

2. _____

3. _____

4. _____

5. _____

6. _____

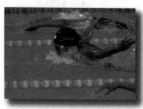

7. _____

B It's Sunday. George is not home. He is at the park. Read about George's day. Complete the sentences. Use the words in the box.

| Go | home | Play | ~~Practice~~ | shower | Watch |

8:00   _____Practice_____ tennis.
        1.

8:30   _____ to the park.
        2.

9:00–12:00 _____ tennis with friends.
            3.

12:00   Go _____.
           4.

12:15   Take a _____.
                5.

12:45   _____ a tennis match on television.
        6.

UNIT 6 GRAMMAR EXERCISES

Grammar to Communicate 1:
Present Progressive: Statements

 A Complete the sentences with the correct form of the verbs.

1. People _____*are running*_____ in the park.
   (run)

2. I _____ right now.
   (work)

3. We _____ track suits.
   (wear)

4. The students _____ English.
   (practice)

5. My mother _____ a shower.
   (take)

6. The boys _____ to school.
   (walk)

B Look at the pictures. Write sentences with the present progressive.

1. _____*The man is running.*_____
   (the man / run)

2. _____*He is not riding a bike.*_____
   (he / not ride / a bike)

3. _____
   (the two women / talk)

4. _____
   (they / not exercise)

5. _____
   (the children / play)

6. _____
   (they / not swim)

7. _____
   (the man / not watch / the children)

8. _____
   (he / sit)

Grammar to Communicate 2:
Present Progressive: *Yes / No* Questions

A **Read the statements. Write questions and short answers.**

1. I'm not eating.

    A: _____ Are you eating? _____   B: _____ No, I'm not. _____

2. They're swimming.

    A: _____   B: _____

3. He's not wearing a helmet.

    A: _____   B: _____

4. She's sitting in the classroom.

    A: _____   B: _____

5. I'm learning English.

    A: _____   B: _____

B **Complete the conversations.**

1. A: Fabrizio is a student.

    B: _____ Is he learning _____ English?
        (he / learn)

    A: Yes, _____ he is _____ .

2. A: Noriko is busy.

    B: _____ today?
        (she / work)

    A: No, _____ . She's exercising.

3. A: Michelle and Henri are at home.

    B: · _____ TV?
        (they / watch)

    A: No, _____ . They're eating.

4. A: I'm on the phone.

    B: _____ to a classmate?
        (you / talk)

    A: Yes, _____ .

Grammar to Communicate 3:
Present Progressive: Information Questions

A Match the questions with the answers. Write the correct letters.

   _c_ **1.** What are you reading?   **a.** An apple.

   _____ **2.** Where is he going?   **b.** To the park.

   _____ **3.** Why is she wearing a helmet?   **c.** A ~~recipe~~.

   _____ **4.** Who are you talking to?   **d.** My best friend.

   _____ **5.** What are you eating?   **e.** Because she is riding her bike.

B Look at the picture. Write present progressive questions.

1. _____ _Where are the children playing?_ _____
   (where / the children / play)

2. _____
   (what / the girl / wear)

3. _____
   (who / she / talk / to)

4. _____
   (what / the boy / do)

5. _____
   (where / the man / sit)

6. _____
   (why / he / watch / TV)

NAME: _____ DATE: _____

Review and Challenge

Complete the phone conversation. Use the words in the box.

are	Is	playing	~~What~~
exercising	'm	riding	Who

Maria: Hi, Tom. This is Maria. Is Yoko there?

Tom: Hi, Maria. No, Yoko isn't here. She's at the college.

Maria: ___What___ is she doing at the college?
   1.

Tom: She's _____ tennis.
   2.

Maria: Good for her! _____ is she playing with?
   3.

Tom: Sylvia. What _____ you doing today? Are you sitting at home?
   4.

Maria: No, I _____ not. I'm _____, too. I'm _____ my bike in
   5.   6.   7.
the park right now.

Tom: Riding and talking on the phone? Be careful! _____ your bike going
   8.
fast?

Maria: Oh, no!

Tom: Maria? Maria! Are you OK? Hello?

UNIT 7 VOCABULARY EXERCISE

Complete the conversations. Use the words in the box.

Ask	~~Finish~~	put	Take	Turn off	wait for
Ask for	move	start	touch	turn on	

1. **Mother:**   Where is your homework?

   Daughter: It's . . . uh . . . well, I . . .

   Mother: ____Finish____ your homework now.

2. **Mary:**   It's 6:00 P.M., and I'm hungry.

   Dad: Please _____ dinner now.

   Mom: Are hamburgers OK?

   Mary and Dad: Great!

3. **Mother:**   Do your homework.

   Son: Mom, please! I'm watching TV.

   Mother: _____ the TV now.

4. **Sister:**   What's for dinner?

   Brother: I don't know. _____ Dad.

5. **Jan:**   I'm making cookies.

   Dan: Mmm!

   Jan: _____ one.

   Dan (*eating*): Mmm! It's good!

6. **Yolanda:**   Is dinner ready?

   Lee: Yes. Just _____ the food on the table.

7. **Olga:** Is the coffee hot?

   Bill: Yes, it is. Don't _____ the cup.

8. **Eric:** I'm thirsty.

   George: Here's the waitress. _____ a glass of water.

9. **Sam:** Is it time for "News Hour"?

   Barbara: Yes. Please _____ the TV.

10. **Ed:** Please _____ the little table.

    Teresa: Where?

    Ed: Next to my chair.

11. **Martha:** Where is Pamela?

    Maria: She's coming. Please _____ her.

UNIT 7 GRAMMAR EXERCISES

Grammar to Communicate 1:
Imperatives

A Write sentences with *Don't*.

1. _____ Don't watch TV. _____ Read a book.
   (watch / TV)

2. _____ Listen.
   (talk)

3. _____ Take the train.
   (take / the bus)

4. _____ Go out and exercise.
   (sit / in your room)

5. _____ Come to the park.
   (go / to the mall)

B Complete the sentences. Use the words in the box. Add *Don't* if necessary. Use capital letters if necessary.

be	listen	run	~~stand~~
eat	open	smoke	take

1. The flight attendant says, "_____ Don't stand _____ in the aisle, please."

2. The teacher says, "Please _____."

3. The doctor says, "_____. It's very bad for your health."

4. The mother says, "_____ your vegetables."

5. The nurse says, "_____ your medicine."

6. The boss says, "_____ late for work."

7. The dentist says, "Please _____ your mouth."

8. The father says, "_____. Walk."

Grammar to Communicate 2: Prepositions

A **Complete the sentences. Circle the correct prepositions.**

1. Put the paper _____ the wastebasket.
   a. in front of   **b. in**

2. Put the wastebasket _____ your desk.
   a. near   **b.** above

3. Put your books _____ your desk.
   a. behind   **b.** on

4. Put the picture _____ your bed.
   a. above   **b.** under

5. Put the rug _____ your bed and your desk.
   a. under   **b.** in

6. Put your clothes _____ the closet.
   a. in   **b.** behind

7. Put your chair _____ your desk.
   a. on   **b.** in front of

B **Maria is talking to her son. Complete her sentences. Use the prepositions *at*, *for*, and *to*.**

1. Wait _for_ me.

2. Listen ____ your teacher.

3. Look ____ the pictures in the book.

4. Be nice ____ your little brother.

5. Ask ____ help.

6. Talk ____ me.

7. Write ____ your grandfather.

8. Wait ____ your brother.

Grammar to Communicate 3:
Object pronouns

A   Complete the sentences. Use *me, you, him, her, it, us,* and *them.*

1. Look for your sister after school. Wait for ____*her*____.

2. Sit with two classmates. Work with _____.

3. Our homework is hard. Please help _____.

4. Wait for me. I'm going with _____.

5. The music is nice. Listen to _____.

6. I'm busy. Don't talk to _____.

7. Your father is going to the store. Go with _____.

B   Complete each conversation. Circle the correct answer and write it on the line.

1. **Jin:**   Filiz and Ismet are here. ____*They*____ are at the door.
   (They / Them)

   Jason: Ask _____ to come in.
   (they / them)

2. **Ana:**   Is Tara there?

   Bill: No, _____ isn't. Tara is at work today. Please call
   (she / her)

   _____ tonight.
   (she / her)

3. **Waiter:**   Here is your fish.

   Customer: It's for my friend. Give it to _____, please. The chicken
   (he / him)

   is for _____.
   (I / me)

   Waiter: The plates are hot. Please don't touch _____.
   (they / them)

   Customer: OK. And please bring _____ some water.
   (we / us)

   Waiter: Sure.

Review and Challenge

Find the mistake in each sentence. Circle the letter and correct the mistake.

1. Please <u>be</u> quiet and <u>listening</u>.
   A   B   Ⓒ

   Correct: _Please be quiet and listen._

2. <u>Wait</u> <u>to</u> the bus <u>on</u> Main Street.
   A   B   C

   Correct: _____

3. <u>No</u> <u>smoke</u> <u>in</u> the building.
   A   B   C

   Correct: _____

4. <u>Talk</u> <u>to</u> Mr. Soto and <u>ask he</u> for help.
   A B   C

   Correct: _____

5. <u>Don't putting</u> your clothes <u>under</u> <u>your bed</u>.
         A   B   C

   Correct: _____

6. <u>Sit down</u> and <u>listen me</u>, <u>please</u>.
     A   B   C

   Correct: _____

7. <u>Put</u> the <u>wastebasket</u> <u>front of</u> the desk.
   A   B   C

   Correct: _____

8. <u>Sitting</u> <u>next to</u> me and help <u>me</u>.
   A   B   C

   Correct: _____

UNIT 8 VOCABULARY EXERCISES

Look at the pictures. What's in the rooms? Write the words next to the numbers of the things in each picture. Use the words in the boxes.

alarm clock	~~keys~~	records
calendar	painting	speakers
camera	radio	
glasses	record player	

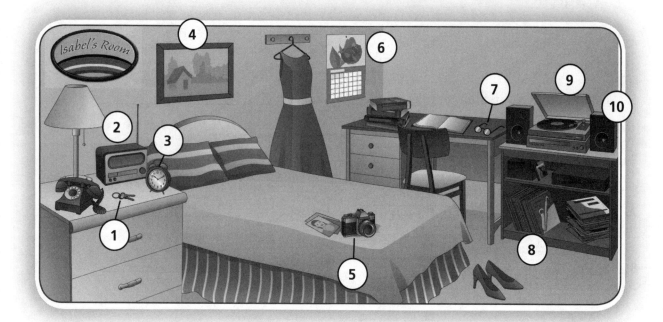

1. __keys_____   6. _____

2. _____   7. _____

3. _____   8. _____

4. _____   9. _____

5. _____   10. _____

CD player	contact lenses	DVDs
CDs	credit card	wallet
cell phone	digital camera	
computer	DVD player	

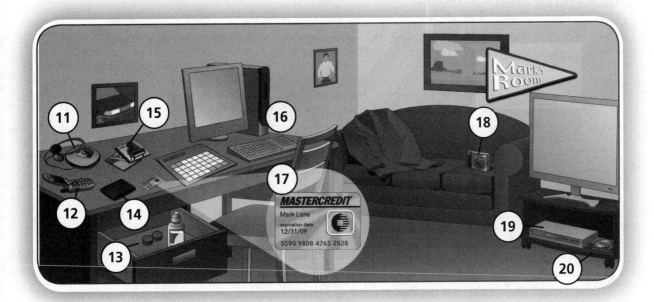

11. _____

12. _____

13. _____

14. _____

15. _____

16. _____

17. _____

18. _____

19. _____

20. _____

UNIT 8 GRAMMAR EXERCISES

Grammar to Communicate 1:
This / That / These / Those

 A Look at the pictures. Complete the sentences with the pronouns *this, that, these,* or *those.* Use *is* or *are.*

1. _____That is_____ an old phone.

5. _____ expensive sunglasses.

2. _____ a cheap necklace.

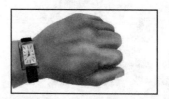

6. _____ a new watch.

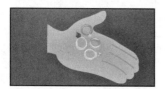

3. _____ nice rings.

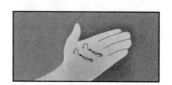

7. _____ pretty earrings.

4. _____ a good radio.

B Rewrite the sentences from Exercise A. Use the adjectives *this, that, these,* or *those.*

1. That phone is old.   5. _____

2. _____   6. _____

3. _____   7. _____

4. _____

Grammar to Communicate 2: Possessive Adjectives and Pronouns

A   **Complete the sentences. Use possessive pronouns.**

1. That's my camera. It's ____mine____.

2. That's Maria's cell phone. It's _____.

3. Those aren't John's keys. They're not _____.

4. These are our books. They're _____.

5. That is their car. It's _____.

6. This is your paper. It's _____.

7. This isn't my watch. It's not _____.

B   **Complete the conversations. Use possessive adjectives or possessive pronouns.**

1. **A:** Is this your cell phone?

    B: Yes, it's ____mine____.

2. **A:** Is that my paper?

    B: No. This is mine. _____ is on the teacher's desk.

3. **A:** Is that their car?

    B: The red car? No. _____ is black.

4. **A:** I'm Paola, and this is _____ husband, Stefano.

    B: It's nice to meet you.

5. **A:** Our son is 7 years old. How old is yours?

    B: _____ is 6, and _____ daughter is 4.

6. **A:** Are these Ana's sunglasses?

    B: No. Those are red. _____ sunglasses are white.

7. **A:** Are these _____ keys?

    B: No, those aren't mine. Maybe they're Wanda's.

Grammar to Communicate 3:
Simple Present: *Have*

A   Complete the sentences. Use *has* or *have.*

1. I _____*have*_____ a new CD.

2. We _____ a big TV.

3. You _____ a nice camera.

4. He _____ a good radio.

5. Carolina _____ a CD player.

6. Ben and Ferdie _____ computers.

7. The school _____ some DVD players.

B   Read the charts. Write sentences about the people. Use *has* or *have.*

NAMES	POSSESSIONS
John	a new computer
Carlos	a digital camera
Marissa	a lot of CDs
Zamir	a new radio

NAMES	POSSESSIONS
Noriko	a lot of CDs
Edgar	a big TV
Laura	two DVD players
Mohammed	a big TV

1. John _____ *has a new computer.* _____

2. Carlos _____

3. Marissa and Noriko _____

4. Zamir _____

5. Edgar and Mohammed _____

6. Laura _____

Review and Challenge

Find the mistake in each conversation. Circle the letter and correct the mistake.

1. **A:** <u>This</u> keys are Jerry's.
    (A)

    B: No. <u>They're</u> <u>mine</u>.
         B   C

    Correct: _These keys are Jerry's._

2. **A:** <u>What's</u> <u>these</u>?
        A   B

    B: <u>That</u> is my new digital camera.
       C

    Correct: _____

3. **A:** Is <u>that</u> Mark's dog?
         A

    B: No. He <u>have</u> a cat. <u>Her</u> name is Daisy.
           B   C

    Correct: _____

4. **A:** Is <u>this</u> <u>your</u> radio?
         A   B

    B: Yes. It's <u>my</u>.
           C

    Correct: _____

5. **A:** <u>That's</u> beautiful earrings.
       A

    B: <u>Thank you</u>. <u>They're</u> new.
        B   C

    Correct: _____

6. **A:** Dina and Rudy <u>has</u> a new car.
               A

    B: Is <u>that</u> <u>their</u> car? It's nice.
         B   C

    Correct: _____

7. **A:** Are <u>these</u> <u>yours</u> books?
          A   B

    B: No. <u>Mine</u> are over there.
         C

    Correct: _____

8. **A:** Marta <u>has</u> a son. <u>His</u> name is Angel.
           A   B

    B: We <u>has</u> a son, too.
         C

    Correct: _____

9. **A:** <u>Are</u> <u>those</u> <u>your</u> children?
       A   B

    B: No. They're <u>ours</u> nephews.
             C

    Correct: _____

UNIT 9 VOCABULARY EXERCISE

Match the sentences. Write the correct letters.

_c_ **1.** Be quiet.

_____ **2.** My friends are in the cafeteria.

_____ **3.** David is at the movie theater. It's 1:00 A.M.

_____ **4.** Amy is a waitress.

_____ **5.** The children are going to school.

_____ **6.** Katie is in the bathroom.

_____ **7.** Dad is having breakfast.

_____ **8.** It's 6:00 A.M. Pedro's alarm clock is loud.

_____ **9.** My aunt is doing housework.

_____ **10.** My uncle is at the library.

a. He's staying out late.

b. He's reading a magazine.

c. ~~The baby is sleeping.~~

d. He's getting up early.

e. She's washing the dishes and doing laundry.

f. He's drinking coffee.

g. She's brushing her teeth.

h. She's working at a café.

i. They're taking the bus.

j. They're having lunch.

UNIT 9 GRAMMAR EXERCISES

Grammar to Communicate 1:
Simple Present: Affirmative Statements

A **Complete the sentences. Circle the correct answers.**

1. My father _____ every day.
   a. work   **(b. works)**

2. My grandmother _____ for our family.
   a. cook   b. cooks

3. I _____ the dishes.
   a. wash   b. washes

4. My parents _____ for a walk in the evening.
   a. go   b. goes

5. My brother _____ on the phone a lot.
   a. talk   b. talks

6. My mother _____ early.
   a. get up   b. gets up

7. My mother and father _____ coffee.
   a. drink   b. drinks

8. I _____ until 8:00 A.M.
   a. sleep   b. sleeps

9. My father _____ to work.
   a. drive   b. drives

B **Complete the story. Use the words in the box.**

~~eat~~	eats	go	play	stays up	works

My brother and I have different routines. I ____*eat*____ dinner at home
                                                1.
every day. He _____ out. I _____ computer games in the evening.
              2.   3.
He _____. I _____ to bed early. He _____ late.
    4.   5.   6.

Grammar to Communicate 2:
Simple Present: Spelling Rules

 Complete the sentences.

1. Ming ____stays____ home in the evening.
   (stay)

2. She _____ with her husband.
   (relax)

3. They _____ TV together.
   (watch)

4. Ann _____ popcorn at the movies.
   (eat)

5. She _____ sad movies.
   (like)

6. She _____ a lot.
   (cry)

7. Lynn _____ a shower every morning.
   (take)

8. She _____ her hair.
   (wash)

9. Lynn _____ long hair.
   (have)

B **Rewrite the sentences. Make the underlined nouns singular.**

1. My <u>brothers</u> wash the dishes.   _My brother washes the dishes._

2. My <u>cousins</u> fix cars.   _____

3. My <u>friends</u> have some computer games. _____

4. My <u>sisters</u> study in the evening.   _____

5. My <u>neighbors</u> finish work at 5:00.   _____

Grammar to Communicate 3:
Simple Present: Negative Statements

 A   **Complete the sentences. Circle the correct verbs.**

1. Dr. Chang drinks tea, but he **(doesn't drink)/ don't drink** coffee.

2. I **doesn't stay up / don't stay up** late during the week.

3. My friends **doesn't work / don't work** on weekends.

4. We **doesn't watch / don't watch** sad movies.

5. Bashir **doesn't have / don't have** a pet.

6. My friends and I **doesn't play / don't play** soccer.

B   **Look at the chart. Complete the sentences about Jim's and Lisa's weekends. Write negative verbs.**

	YES	NO
Jim	play tennis eat out go to bed early	work study cook
Lisa	watch soccer eat out stay up late	work study play soccer

1. Jim and Lisa _____don't work_____ on weekends. They relax.

2. They study during the week. They _____ on weekends.

3. Lisa watches soccer on TV, but she _____ soccer.

4. Jim plays tennis. He _____ tennis on TV.

5. Jim and Lisa eat out on weekends. They _____ dinner at home.

6. Jim cooks during the week, but he _____ on weekends.

7. Jim goes to bed early. He _____ late.

8. Lisa _____ to bed early. She stays up late.

Review and Challenge

Correct the conversation. There are ten mistakes. The first mistake is corrected for you.

Luisa: Hello, Slava. Is Natalya there?

Slava: No, she isn't. She ~~work~~ *works* from 3:00 to 11:00 on Tuesdays.

Luisa: Is she home on Wednesdays?

Slava: Well, she don't work, but she go to school.

Luisa: What time?

Slava: Her first class start at 9:00. She isn't drive—she take the bus—so she leave at 8:10. Call her between 7:30 and 8:00.

Luisa: I no get up until 9:00 or 10:00. My classes doesn't start until 11:00.

Slava: Call her in the afternoon, then. She study at home in the afternoon.

NAME: _____ DATE: _____

UNIT 10 VOCABULARY EXERCISES

Complete the conversations. Use the words in the boxes.

| 25 percent off | ~~department store~~ | pay for | sell |
| cash | on sale | receipt | spending money on |

Tony works at Murray's Department Store. Eric and Katie are shopping there.

Kate: This is a good ___department store___.
1.

Eric: Yes, it is. . . . Oh, excuse me. Do you _____ DVD players?
2.

Tony: Yes, we do.

Eric: Are there any DVD players _____?
3.

Tony: Yes, this DVD player is _____. It's a new player from
4.

France.

Eric: $159.00. Hmmm . . .

Katie: Why are you _____ a new DVD player?
5.

Eric: It's for my mother. It's her birthday.

Katie: Oh, OK.

Tony: How will you _____ this?
6.

Eric: With _____.
7.

Tony: Thank you. Here's your _____.
8.

| closes | convenience store | opens |

(On the street)

Eric: Is there a _____ near here?
9.

Katie: There's a store here on Washington Street.

Eric: It isn't open now. It _____ at 11:00, and it's 11:05 now.
10.

Katie: Oh, well. Wait for morning. The store _____ at 6:00 A.M.
11.

UNIT 10 GRAMMAR EXERCISES

Grammar to Communicate 1:
Frequency Adverbs

A Rewrite the sentences. Add the adverbs.

1. I use credit cards. _____ I usually use credit cards. _____
    (usually)

2. I use cash in stores. _____
    (hardly ever)

3. That convenience store is open. _____
    (always)

4. Malls are open on holidays. _____
    (sometimes)

5. We go shopping on weekends. _____
    (often)

6. My friends shop at the mall. _____
    (never)

B Look at the chart. Complete the sentences about the three stores.

	A.J.'s	McNabb's	Orlov's
Stays open late	sometimes	usually	always
Is open on Sundays	never	always	always
Has good sales	hardly ever	sometimes	often

1. A.J.'s Department Store _____ sometimes stays open late. _____

2. It _____ is never open on Sundays. _____

3. It _____

4. McNabb's Department Store _____

5. It _____

6. It _____

7. Orlov's Department Store _____

8. It _____

9. It _____

Grammar to Communicate 2:
Simple Present: *Yes/No* questions

A Write questions and complete the short answers.

1. ____Do the children need new shoes?____   Yes, ___they do___ .
   (the children / need / new shoes)

2. _____   Yes, _____ .
   (Bob and Mary / want / a new TV)

3. _____   No, _____ .
   (I / need / a tie)

4. _____   Yes, _____ .
   (Anthony / want / a car)

5. _____   Yes, _____ .
   (Maria / like / expensive clothes)

6. _____   No, _____ .
   (you / spend / a lot on clothes)

B Look at the chart. Write questions with *have*. Then write true answers.

you / your friend	a cell phone	a new computer	an old car

1. A: _____Do you have a cell phone?_____

   B: _____Yes, I do. OR No, I don't._____

2. A: _____Does your friend have a cell phone?_____

   B: _____Yes, he/she does. OR No, he/she doesn't._____

3. A: _____

   B: _____

4. A: _____

   B: _____

5. A: _____

   B: _____

6. A: _____

   B: _____

Grammar to Communicate 3:
Simple Present: Information Questions

 A **Complete the questions. Circle the correct words.**

1. (What time)/ How often does the electronics store open?

2. What / What kind of do you need at the electronics store?

3. How much / What kind of TVs do they sell?

4. How much / How often do you want to spend?

5. What time / How often do you buy a new TV?

B **Complete the conversations. Write information questions. Use *What, What kind of, What time, How often,* and *How much.***

1. **A:** That store stays open late.

   B: _____What time does it close?_____
                        (it / close)

   A: 11:00 P.M.

2. **A:** _____
                        (they /sell)

   B: They sell clothes and jewelry.

3. **A:** _____
                        (the supermarket / open)

   B: At 7:00 A.M.

4. **A:** _____
                        (you / go shopping)

   B: I go every weekend.

5. **A:** Those are nice earrings. _____
                                                    (they / cost)

   B: They're $22.00.

6. **A:** Anna never wears necklaces.

   B: _____
                        (jewelry / she / wear)

   A: She likes earrings and bracelets.

Review and Challenge

Correct the conversation. There are eight mistakes. The first mistake is corrected for you.

Karen: Do you ever shop at the Springfield Mall?

Liz: Sure. ~~Often I~~ I often go there.

Karen: What time the stores open?

Liz: Well, I go usually there on Sundays, and on Sundays they open at 10:00.

Karen: What kind things do you buy at the mall?

Liz: I like the clothes at Bettie's. I like Dave's Sporting Goods, too. What you need at the mall?

Karen: Some new clothes. Does Bettie's has good prices?

Liz: Yes. They have always great prices. Come with me this Sunday.

Karen: OK, thanks. What time?

Liz: How about 10:30? No, wait—make that 10:00. Never you are ready on time!

UNIT 11 VOCABULARY EXERCISES

A   Read the invitation. Answer the questions. Use complete sentences.

Gloria and Edward Miller
10 Lake Drive
Los Angeles, CA 99999

Ms. Elizabeth Miller
400 Lincoln Street
Pasadena, CA 99999

Gloria and Edward Miller invite you and a guest
to the wedding of their daughter,
Miss Jane Miller,
and
Mr. John Torres,
on August 16th
at the Grand Hotel.

1. Who is the bride?   _____Jane Miller is the bride._____

2. Who is the groom?   _____

3. Who is the hostess?   _____

4. Who is the host?   _____

5. Who is the invitation for?   _____

6. Is this invitation for a birthday party?   _____

7. Elizabeth Miller wants to invite a
   guest. Is it OK?   _____

B **Complete the story. Use the words in the box.**

Birthday	dance	give me gifts	invite	thank
celebrate	flowers	have a party	makes a cake	visit

My _____Birthday_____
                    1.

I always _____ my birthday with my family and friends.
                    2.

I get _____ from my father. He puts them on the table in my
            3.

bedroom. My mother _____. She usually makes a carrot cake. That's
                            4.

my favorite. In the afternoon, I _____. I _____
                                    5.   6.

my friends to swim in my pool. We play music and _____. We
                                                        7.

eat birthday cake. Then my friends _____. I open them, and
                                            8.

I _____ everyone for the wonderful things. In the evening, I
        9.

_____ my grandmother. My family and I have a special party with
            10.

her. We have dinner and talk all night.

UNIT 11 GRAMMAR EXERCISES

Grammar to Communicate 1:
Direct and Indirect Objects

A Complete the conversation. Write *to* or *for*.

Anya: Do you usually give birthday presents _____to_____ your friends?
1.

Ruth: No, but I always send birthday cards _____ my friends and
2.
family.

Anya: Do you buy flowers _____ them?
3.

Ruth: Sometimes I get flowers _____ them from my garden. How
4.
about you? What do you give _____ your friends on their
5.
birthdays?

Anya: I like to make gifts _____ my friends.
6.

B Rewrite the sentences in Exercise A. Do not use *to* or *for*.

1. Do you usually give your friends birthday presents?

2. _____

3. _____

4. _____

5. _____

6. _____

Grammar to Communicate 2:
Simple Present: Information Questions

A Write questions. Put the words in the correct order. Add *Do* or *Does.*

1. _____How does your family celebrate Memorial Day?_____
   (how / celebrate / your family / Memorial Day)

2. _____
   (Thanksgiving / when / Canadians / celebrate)

3. _____
   (Americans / why / July Fourth / celebrate)

4. _____
   (how / people / celebrate / Father's Day)

5. _____
   (New Year's Eve / your family / celebrate / where)

6. _____
   (when / Americans / Labor Day / celebrate)

B Read the answers about Mother's Day and Father's Day. Then write questions with *When, Where, How,* and *Why.*

1. **A:** _____When do you celebrate Mother's Day?_____

   B: On the second Sunday in May.

2. **A:** _____

   B: We celebrate at home.

3. **A:** _____

   B: We have a nice dinner, and we give our mother cards and gifts.

4. **A:** _____

   B: Because we love our mother!

5. **A:** _____

   B: We celebrate Father's Day on the third Sunday in June.

Grammar to Communicate 3:
Who as Subject and Object

A   Underline the subjects of the sentences. Then write questions with *Who.*

1. <u>My children</u> love birthdays.

    Who loves birthdays? _____

2. I plan birthday parties for them.

    _____

3. My children make the invitations.

    _____

4. Their friends bring gifts.

    _____

5. The children play games at their birthday parties.

    _____

6. I make the birthday cake.

    _____

B   Circle the objects of the sentences. Write questions with *who* and *do.* Then write the answers.

1. We invite (our friends) on New Year's Eve.

    A: *Who do you invite on New Year's Eve?*   **B:** _*Our friends.*_

2. I call my friends on their birthdays.

    A: _____   **B:** _____

3. Americans celebrate mothers on Mother's Day.

    A: _____   **B:** _____

4. Children visit their neighbors on Halloween.

    A: _____   **B:** _____

5. Americans celebrate workers on Labor Day.

    A: _____   **B:** _____

6. People invite relatives and friends to holiday parties.

    A: _____   **B:** _____

Review and Challenge

Complete the conversation. Use the words in the box.

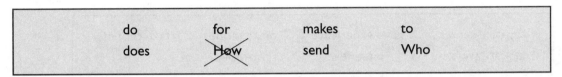

do	for	makes	to
does	~~How~~	send	Who

June: _____How_____ do you celebrate your wife's birthday?
1.

Mark: I usually buy flowers _____ her. And we go out to eat.
2.

June: How _____ your wife celebrate your birthday?
3.

Mark: She always gets me a nice present, and she _____ a cake for me.
4.

June: _____ sends you cards on your birthdays?
5.

Mark: Our friends and relatives _____.
6.

June: Do you _____ cards to them, too?
7.

Mark: Of course. And we give gifts and cards _____ our children on their
8.

birthdays.

UNIT 12 VOCABULARY EXERCISES

A Complete the conversation. Use the words in the box.

day-care center	have experience	make money	take care of
day-care worker	~~Interview~~	manager	

A Job _____Interview_____
                    1.

Mr. Lopez: Good morning. I'm Carlos Lopez, the _____ of
                    2.

SuperKids Day-Care Center.

Ms. Yang: Nice to meet you. I'm Mei-Li Yang.

Mr. Lopez: Please sit down. Now, then . . . Do you _____ with
                    3.

children?

Ms. Yang: Oh, yes. I'm a _____ at Little Friends now.
                    4.

Mr. Lopez: What is Little Friends?

Ms. Yang: Little Friends is a _____, too. I sometimes
                    5.

_____ children in the evening to
              6

_____.
        7.

Mr. Lopez: Why do you want to change jobs?

Ms. Yang: I work in the mornings, but I want to work mornings and afternoons.

Mr. Lopez: Good. I need someone to work in the afternoons. Are you ready to

start Monday?

Ms. Yang: Yes, I am.

Mr. Lopez: Great! Welcome to SuperKids.

Ms. Yang: Thank you for the job, Mr. Lopez.

B **Complete the conversations. Use the words in the box.**

| am off   co-worker   make an appointment   paychecks   real estate agent |

1. **Dana:** Inez has a new job.

   Tim: I know. She sells houses. She's a _____.

2. **Tim:** Marie, the boss has our _____.

   Marie: Oh, thanks. It's Friday! I need my money.

3. **Inez:** Tim, this is Akiko. Akiko, this is Tim. I work with Akiko. She's my

   _____.

   Tim: Nice to meet you, Akiko.

4. **Inez:** I don't work on Mondays. I _____ Mondays.

   Marie: That's nice!

5. *[On the telephone]*

   Nan: Good morning. Doctor Green's office.

   Polly: Good morning. I want to _____ with Dr. Green. Is
   next Wednesday at 2:00 OK?

   Nan: Yes, that's fine.

UNIT 12 GRAMMAR EXERCISES

Grammar to Communicate 1:
Simple Present and Present Progressive

 A   Look at the pictures. Complete the questions. Then complete the answers.

1. Is the woman __brushing__ her teeth?   Yes, __she is__ .
    (brush)

2. Does she __brush__ her teeth every day?   Yes, __she does__ .
    (brush)

3. Is the man _____ dinner?   No, _____ .
    (have)

4. Does he always _____ lunch at home?   Yes, _____ .
    (eat)

5. Do the men _____ in an office?   No, _____ .
    (work)

6. Are they _____ now?   Yes, _____ .
    (work)

B   Read the questions about Jack. Circle the correct answers.

1. What does Jack do?

    a. He's a real estate agent.   **b.** He's talking to a customer.

2. What does he do every day?

    a. He sells houses.   **b.** He's selling a house.

3. What is he doing now?

    a. He shows houses to buyers.   **b.** He's showing a house to a buyer.

4. Is he working in his office now?

    a. No, he doesn't.   **b.** No, he isn't.

5. Does he sell apartment buildings and office buildings?

    a. No, he doesn't.   **b.** No, he isn't.

6. Does he work hard at his job?

    a. Yes, he does.   **b.** Yes, he is.

Grammar to Communicate 2:
Stative Verbs

A   **Complete the sentences. Use the simple present or the present progressive.**

1.   I _____*see*_____ the secretary. She's talking on the phone.
        (see)

2.   Rita _____ this evening. She always works evenings.
              (work)

3.   My co-worker is talking to the manager. I _____ them.
                                                     (hear)

4.   Arturo is working hard. He is tired. He _____ a break.
                                                  (need)

5.   The directions are easy. We _____ them.
                                    (understand)

6.   You _____ an excellent job now. Keep up the good work!
           (do)

7.   I _____ the mechanics. I don't know their boss.
         (know)

8.   Jackie's new secretary is nice. Jackie _____ her.
                                                (like)

9.   I usually have soup for lunch. Today I _____ a sandwich.
                                               (want)

B   **Write sentences. Use the simple present or the present progressive.**

1.   _____My co-workers like music._____
                          (my co-workers / like / music)

2.   _____
                          (they / listen / to the radio / now)

3.   _____
                          (I / not / like / their music)

4.   _____
                          (the boss / not / want / the radio on)

5.   _____
                          (she / turn off / the radio / now)

6.   _____
                          (my co-workers / not / understand)

Grammar to Communicate 3:
Like / Need / Want + Infinitive

 A   Circle the seven infinitives in the conversation. The first infinitive is circled for you.

Alex: The boss wants (to talk) to you.

Bella: To me? Why does he want to talk to me?

Alex: He needs to ask you about the schedule. He wants to make some changes. He likes to talk to people first.

Bella: I like the schedule now. I don't want to change.

Alex: Talk to the boss about it. You need to go to his office.

B   Write sentences about yourself. Write negative sentences where necessary.

1.   <u>I want to be a teacher. OR I don't want to be a teacher.</u>
   (want / be / a teacher)

2.   _____
   (need / find / a job)

3.   _____
   (like / do / office work)

4.   _____
   (want / learn / about computers)

5.   _____
   (need / get / a college degree)

6.   _____
   (like / learn / new things)

7.   _____
   (want / move / a different country)

Review and Challenge

Find the mistake in each sentence. Circle the letter and correct the mistake.

1. <u>What</u> <u>is your wife</u> do?
    A   (B)   C

    Correct: _What does your wife do?_

2. <u>Be</u> the <u>manager</u> <u>working</u> today?
    A   B   C

    Correct: _____

3. <u>My co-worker</u> <u>wants</u> <u>to gets</u> a new job.
        A   B   C

    Correct: _____

4. <u>Are you needing</u> a <u>day off</u> <u>this weekend</u>?
          A   B   C

    Correct: _____

5. Please <u>be</u> quiet. I <u>listen</u> <u>to the directions.</u>
           A   B   C

    Correct: _____

6. <u>The boss</u> <u>is understanding</u> <u>the problems.</u>
       A   B   C

    Correct: _____

7. <u>Do</u> you <u>need</u> <u>making</u> a lot of money?
    A   B   C

    Correct: _____

8. <u>What</u> <u>is</u> he <u>do</u> in his office every day?
    A   B   C

    Correct: _____

9. He <u>doesn't</u> <u>want</u> <u>being</u> a real estate agent.
        A   B   C

    Correct: _____

10. <u>Is</u> she <u>answer</u> the phone <u>every</u> day?
    A   B   C

    Correct: _____

UNIT 13 VOCABULARY EXERCISES

Look at the pictures. Complete the stories. Use the words in the boxes.

| ~~crowded~~ | in a good mood | noisy | slow | wonderful | worried |

A Restaurant Review

Many people go to Hector's Café on Saturday night. It is usually

_____crowded_____. The service is _____, but the food is
            1.   2.
_____. Hector's Café isn't quiet. It's _____.
            3.   4.
People are _____ at Hector's. But the food is expensive. Don't go to
                        5.
Hector's if you are _____ about money. Go to Hector's when you
                                    6.
have a lot of time and a lot of money!

angry	dirty	rude	terrible
clean	in a bad mood	service	

A Hotel Review

The Ramsey Hotel is not a nice hotel. The rooms aren't _____.
7.
They are _____. Some of the hotel workers are
8.
_____ to the guests. The workers are _____
9.   10.
because they want to make more money. Don't go to the Ramsey Hotel. The
_____ isn't good. In fact, it's _____! That's why
11.   12.
the guests at the Ramsey Hotel are always _____.
13.

UNIT 13 GRAMMAR EXERCISES

Grammar to Communicate 1:
Simple Past of *Be:* Statements

A **Complete the sentences about last week. Use *was* or *were*.**

1. My family _____was_____ on vacation last week.

2. We _____ at the beach.

3. My children _____ happy.

4. Their schools _____ closed all week.

5. The weather _____ great.

6. I _____ in a good mood all week.

B **Complete the story. Circle the correct answer and write it on the line.**

LAST WEEK

Last week _____was_____ a busy week at school.
1. (was / were)

There _____ tests on Tuesday, Wednesday, and
2. (was / were)

Thursday. The students _____ in a good mood.
3. (wasn't / weren't)

Then on Friday, there _____ a big party at school.
4. (was / were)

There _____ a lot of people at the party. We
5. (was / were)

_____ happy because it _____
6. (was / were)   7. (was / were)

Friday. There _____ good food at the party. There
8. (was / were)

_____ any homework that night.
3. (wasn't / weren't)

Grammar to Communicate 2:
Simple Past of *Be: Yes / No* Questions

A **Match the questions about last night with the answers. Write the correct letters.**

_c_ **1.** Were there a lot of people at the restaurant?   **a.** Yes, I was.

____ **2.** Was there a long wait for a table?   **b.** Yes, it was.

____ **3.** Was the food good?   **c.** Yes, ~~there~~ were.

____ **4.** Were the waiters polite?   **d.** No, there wasn't.

____ **5.** Were you happy with the service?   **e.** Yes, they were.

B **Write questions. Put the words in the correct order. Use *Was* or *Were*. Then complete the answers.**

1. A: ___Was your shopping trip good?_____
         (good / shopping trip / your)
   B: Yes, ___it was_____.

2. A: _____
         (crowded / the stores)
   B: No, they _____.

3. A: _____
         (a lot of / there / people)
   B: No, there _____.

4. A: _____
         (good / the prices)
   B: Yes, they _____.

5. A: _____
         (there / things on sale / a lot of)
   B: Yes, there _____.

6. A: _____
         (busy / the salespeople)
   B: No, they _____.

Grammar to Communicate 3:
Simple Past of *Be:* Information Questions

A   Read the answers. Write questions. Use *When, Why, How,* or *Where* and the correct form of *be.*

1.   **A:** _____ How was the weather? _____

     B: The weather was pretty good.

2.   **A:** _____

     B: The test was yesterday.

3.   **A:** _____

     B: I was home from work because I was sick.

4.   **A:** _____

     B: The party was at David's house.

5.   **A:** _____

     B: My vacation was wonderful.

B   Write questions with *Who* about yesterday's lunch. Ask about the underlined words.

1.   **A:** I was with <u>Nina</u> at lunch yesterday.

     B: Who were you with at lunch yesterday?

     A: Nina.

2.   **A:** <u>Jorge</u> was at the restaurant.

     B: _____

     A: Jorge was.

3.   **A:** Jorge was with <u>Carolina</u>.

     B: _____

     A: Carolina.

4.   **A:** <u>Carolina</u> was on the phone a lot.

     B: _____

     A: Carolina was.

5.   **A:** <u>Our waiter</u> was really slow.

     B: _____

     A: Our waiter was.

6.   **A:** Nina was mad at <u>our waiter</u>.

     B: _____

     A: Our waiter.

Review and Challenge

Correct the conversation. There are ten mistakes. The first mistake is corrected for you.

Olga: My family and I ~~was~~ *were* on vacation last week.

Leslie: Where you were?

Olga: At the beach. It was great.

Leslie: Who was the weather?

Olga: It was really nice.

Leslie: Was you at a hotel?

Olga: No, we with Alex, at his house.

Leslie: Who you with?

Olga: Alex—you know, my cousin.

Leslie: Oh, yes. I remember him. The house was it nice?

Olga: Yes, it was, and it was only about five minutes from the beach.

Leslie: Was crowded the beach?

Olga: No, there wasn't. There were no a lot of people.

UNIT 14 VOCABULARY EXERCISE

Complete the story. Use the words in the box.

catch	chases	~~gets out~~	leave	scream
change	forget	happens	lose	Take ... back

My dog Fred is very bad. He ___gets out___ of the house every morning. I don't
                                         1.

know how. I never _____ to close the door, but Fred runs out. He _____
                              2.   3.

the neighbor's cat and makes a lot of noise. The neighbors _____, "_____
                                                                  4.   5.

that dog _____ into your house!" So then I run after Fred and _____ him. I
                                                                           6.

put him back in the house. When I _____ the house and go to work, Fred is sad.
                                         7.

Fred is very intelligent. A funny thing _____ when I _____ my keys. I
                                               8.   9.

say to Fred, "Keys!" and Fred runs around the house. He always finds my keys. When I

say to Fred, "Cat!" he runs to the door. He opens it with his mouth and runs out. I don't

need a new dog. I need to _____ my door!
                                10.

UNIT 14 GRAMMAR EXERCISES

Grammar to Communicate 1:
Simple Past: Regular Verbs

A **Complete the sentences. Use the words in the box.**

arrived	called	~~cleaned~~	cooked	invited	listened

Saturday was a busy day for me. In the morning, I ___cleaned___ my
                                                          1.
apartment. Then I picked up the phone and _____ my friends. I
                                                    2.
_____ them to dinner. I was in the kitchen all afternoon. I _____
   3.   **4.**
a lot of food, and I _____ to the radio. My friends _____ at 6:00
                          5.   **6.**
P.M. It was a really nice evening.

B **Read the charts about daily activities. Write sentences about yesterday.**

1	Marta	work
2	I	wash dishes
3	Leo	study
4	we	wait for the bus

5	Barbara	watch the news
6	Ari	play tennis
7	our class	start at 9:00 A.M.
8	the bank	close at 5:00 P.M.

1. ___Marta worked yesterday._____

2. _____

3. _____

4. _____

5. _____

6. _____

7. _____

8. _____

Grammar to Communicate 2:
Simple Past: Irregular Verbs

A **Complete the sentences. Use the simple past.**

1. I _____ got up _____ at 7:00 A.M. today.
        (get up)

2. Jack _____ two miles yesterday.
              (run)

3. Oh, no! I _____ my homework.
                (forget)

4. The baby _____ her milk.
                  (drink)

5. My grandmother _____ me a letter.
                        (write)

6. I _____ the phone.
         (hear)

7. All the students _____ the answer.
                          (know)

8. Miranda _____ her keys.
                  (lose)

B **Complete the story. Use the simple past.**

Last year, the Lombardellis ___ moved ___ from New York to Florida.
                                  1. (move)

They _____ a lot of furniture, so they needed help. They _____
        2. (have)   3. (call)

ACE Movers. The movers _____ to the house. The men _____ the
                            4. (come)   5. (spend)

day at the Lombardellis' house. They _____ their furniture to Florida.
                                          6. (take)

The Lombardellis were happy with ACE Movers. The movers _____ a
                                                              7. (do)

good job.

Grammar to Communicate 3:
Simple Past: Negative Statements

 A   The affirmative statements on the left are false. Write negative statements to make them true.

FALSE!	TRUE!
1. Ali went to the beach.	1. Ali didn't go to the beach.
2. I worked all night.	2.
3. Marcia woke up late.	3.
4. We made a lot of mistakes.	4.
5. Ben drank ten cups of tea.	5.
6. Lisa washed the car.	6.
7. They invited us to their wedding.	7.
8. You ate breakfast in class.	8.

B   Complete the story. Write negative statements. Use the words in the box.

go out	~~have~~	like	play	sleep	spend

I _____didn't have_____ a good vacation. The weather was really
                1.

bad. We _____ tennis. We _____ time
                2.   3.

at the beach. The restaurants were expensive. We _____
                                                        4.

to eat very often. We _____ our hotel. The beds were
                            5.

uncomfortable. We _____ well. I'm glad to be home.
                        6.

Review and Challenge

Complete the conversation. Use the words in the box.

came	left	saw	was
didn't	made	talk	went
~~heard~~	said	talked	

Ted: I ___*heard*___ a funny story this morning.
      1.

Alice: Tell me about it.

Ted: A man _____ to the store with a friend. They drove there in her
      2.

car—a small, blue car. They _____ the car in a crowded parking lot.
      3.

The woman went into the supermarket, and the man went into another

store. Then he went back to the car and got in to wait. But he _____ a
      4.

mistake. It _____ a different small, blue car—not his friend's car.
    5.

Alice: Uh-oh!

Ted: An old woman _____ out of the supermarket. She _____ a man
      6.   **7.**

sitting in her small, blue car. She was scared because she _____ know
      8.

the man. She didn't _____ to him. She called the police.
    9.

Alice: Did the police come?

Ted: Yes, and they _____ to the man. He _____, "Sorry!"
      10.   **11.**

UNIT 15 VOCABULARY EXERCISE

Complete the sentences. Use the words in the box.

are in the military	get a driver's license	get married	~~have a baby~~	meet
become a citizen	get a job	graduate	have an accident	retire

1. Your friends say, "Congratulations! Is it a boy or a girl?" when you
   _____*have a baby*_____.

2. You wear special clothes and cut your hair when you _____.

3. You say to your parents, "I need the car, please" when you

   _____.

4. You don't go to work when you _____. You stay at home.

5. You become a husband or a wife when you _____.

6. Your friends ask, "Are you OK?" when you _____.

7. You study for four years at a university, and then you _____.

8. You say hello and say your name when you _____ a person for
   the first time.

9. Your boss says, "Don't be late!" when you _____.

10. If you move to a new country, sometimes you _____ of the new
    country.

UNIT 15 GRAMMAR EXERCISES

Grammar to Communicate 1:
Simple Past: *Yes/No* questions

A Complete the questions about last weekend. Then write true answers.

1. _Did you take a trip_ last weekend?   Yes, I did. OR No, I didn't.
    (you / take / a trip)

2. _Was the weather nice_ on Saturday?   Yes, it was. OR No, it wasn't.
    (the weather / be / nice)

3. _____ homework?   _____
    (you and your class / have)

4. _____ on the weekend?   _____
    (you / see / your friends)

5. _____ together?   _____
    (you and your friends / do / things)

6. _____ for you?   _____
    (it / be / a good weekend)

B Complete the questions. Use *was*, *were*, or *did*. Then write true answers.

When you were a child, . . .

1. . . . _did_ did you live in the city?   Yes, I did. OR No, I didn't.

2. . . . _were_ you a good student?   Yes, I was. OR No, I wasn't.

3. . . . _____ you take the bus to school?   _____

4. . . . _____ you like school?   _____

5. . . . _____ school easy for you?   _____

6. . . . _____ you have a lot of homework?   _____

7. . . . _____ your classes big?   _____

8. . . . _____ you have a lot of friends at school? _____

Grammar to Communicate 2:
Simple Past: Information Questions; Information Questions with *Who* and *What* as Subject

A   Complete the questions.

1. When _____ did you get your first job? _____
    (you / get / your first job)

2. Where _____
    (you / work)

3. What kind of _____
    (job / you / have)

4. How _____
    (you / find / the job)

5. Why _____
    (you / leave / the job)

6. What _____
    (you / do / after that)

B   Read the answers. Then write questions about the underlined words. Use *What, Where, When, How old,* or *Who*.

1. **A:** _____ When did Carlos start school? _____

    B: Carlos started school in 1993.

2. **A:** _____

    B: He was 5 years old.

3. **A:** _____

    B: He went to school in Santo Domingo.

4. **A:** _____

    B: His mother took him to school every day.

5. **A:** _____

    B: He carried a backpack on his back.

6. **A:** _____

    B: His first teacher was his neighbor.

Grammar to Communicate 3:
How long ago / How long

A   Complete the sentences with *for* or *ago*.

1. I moved here a year _____ago_____.

2. I worked at my last job _____ two years.

3. The class ended an hour _____.

4. I was in high school _____ four years.

5. I waited for you _____ 20 minutes.

6. My grandfather was born 82 years _____.

7. They got married a month _____.

B   Write questions. Use *How long* or *How long ago*.

1. A: _____ How long ago did you start learning English? _____
   (you / start / learning English)

   B: Ten months ago.

2. A: _____
   (they / get / married)

   B: A year ago.

3. A: _____
   (they / stay / married)

   B: Only a month.

4. A: _____
   (you and your wife / meet)

   B: About 12 years ago.

5. A: _____
   (you / stay / at your first job)

   B: Three months.

6. A: _____
   (they / build / our school)

   B: More than 100 years ago.

Review and Challenge

Find the mistake in each conversation. Circle the letter and correct the mistake.

1. **A:** <u>Did</u> you <u>had</u> fun at the party?
     A   (B)

   B: Yes, we <u>did</u>.
           C

   Correct: *Did you have fun at the party?*

2. **A:** <u>Did</u> you <u>finish</u> high school?
     A   B

   B: Yes, I <u>was</u>.
         C

   Correct: _____

3. **A:** <u>Were</u> you <u>live</u> there a long time?
     A   B

   B: Yes, <u>for</u> 20 years.
         C

   Correct: _____

4. **A:** <u>Were</u> you a quiet <u>child</u>?
     A   B

   B: No, I <u>didn't</u>.
         C

   Correct: _____

5. **A:** <u>What kind of</u> movie <u>you saw</u>?
     A   B

   B: <u>We went to</u> an action movie.
        C

   Correct: _____

6. **A:** <u>What</u> <u>was happen</u> in class yesterday?
     A   B

   B: We <u>had</u> a test.
         C

   Correct: _____

7. **A:** <u>Who</u> <u>give</u> you <u>those flowers</u>?
     A B   C

   B: My sister did.

   Correct: _____

8. **A:** <u>How long</u> <u>ago</u> <u>you met</u> your husband?
        A   B   C

   B: Fifteen years ago.

   Correct: _____

9. **A:** <u>How</u> <u>long ago</u> did you <u>stay</u> at the party?
        A   B   C

   B: About two hours.

   Correct: _____

10. **A:** <u>When</u> <u>did</u> they get married?
         A   B

    B: <u>For 32 years</u>.
          C

    Correct: _____

NAME: _____   DATE: _____

UNIT 16 VOCABULARY EXERCISE

Complete the letter. Use the words in the box.

buy groceries	have friends over	pick up	stay at home	tonight
go on a picnic	~~leave the house~~	play cards	take	

Hi, Annie!

    I got a new job! I live with the Bennett family and take care of the children,

Bonnie and Ryan. In the morning, Mr. and Mrs. Bennett _____*leave the house*_____

                                                  1.

at 8:00. They _____ Bonnie to school. Ryan doesn't go to
                                2.

school. He's two years old. Ryan and I _____ and play in his
                                            3.

room. Sometimes I _____ at the supermarket, and I make
                              4.

lunch. In the afternoon, I _____ Bonnie from school. The
                              5.

children and I go to the park and play. Sometimes I make sandwiches, and we

_____ in the park. At 6:00, Mr. and Mrs. Bennett come home.
                6.

In the evenings, I usually go out with my friends, but _____
                                                            7.

I am staying at home. I like to _____ sometimes. We
                                8.

_____ or watch TV.
         9.

Take care,

Jen

UNIT 16 GRAMMAR EXERCISES

Grammar to Communicate 1:
Be going to: Statements

A   **Complete the story. Use *be going to*.**

It _____*is going to be*_____ warm and sunny this weekend.

1. (be)

On Saturday, my friends and I _____ to the

2. (go)

park. I _____ sandwiches for a picnic. Mei Li

3. (make)

_____ a salad. Hiro and Yoshi _____

4. (bring)   5. (get)

some drinks and dessert. They _____ tennis at the park.

6. (play)

We _____ a nice time.

7. (have)

B   **Look at the weather chart. Complete the sentences about the weather tomorrow. Use negative forms where necessary.**

City	Today	F/C	Tomorrow	F/C
Beijing	☁	61/16°	🌬☀	62/17°
Mexico City	☀	81/27°	☀	81/27°
Moscow	❄🌬	32/0°	❄	38/3°
São Paulo	☁	90/32°	☁	88/31°
Toronto	🌧	46/8°	🌧	51/10°
Weather Chart Key				
windy = 🌬		cloudy = ☁		sunny = ☀
humid = ☁		snow = ❄		rain = 🌧

1.   (be) _____*It's going to be*_____ sunny and windy in Beijing tomorrow.

2.   (rain) _____ in Beijing.

3.   (be) _____ sunny in Mexico City tomorrow.

4.   (be) _____ cloudy in Mexico City.

5.   (snow) _____ in Moscow tomorrow.

6.   (rain) _____ in Moscow.

7.   (be) _____ hot and humid in São Paulo tomorrow.

8.   (snow) _____ in São Paulo.

Grammar to Communicate 2:
Be going to: Yes/No questions

A **Complete the sentences. Circle the correct answers.**

1. Are you going to go out _____ evening?
    a. tomorrow   b. next

2. Are we going to be late _____ morning?
    a. next   b. this

3. Is there going to be a test _____ week?
    a. this   b. tomorrow

4. Are the children going to be home _____ night?
    a. next   b. tomorrow

5. Is Will going to find a job _____?
    a. soon   b. yesterday

6. Is it going to rain _____?
    a. last night   b. tonight

B **Write questions. Use *be going to*.**

1. _____Are they going to go out this evening?_____
    (they / go out / this evening)

2. _____
    (there / be / a party / this weekend)

3. _____
    (we / have / homework / tonight)

4. _____
    (the weather / be / nice / tomorrow)

5. _____
    (there / be / many people / at the wedding)

6. _____
    (the doctor / call / later)

7. _____
    (you / go / to the mall / soon)

8. _____
    (I / miss / the bus)

Grammar to Communicate 3:
Be going to: Information Questions

A Write questions about Joe and Judy's plans. Use the correct form of *be going to.*

1. A: _____Who is going to get married?_____   B: Joe and Judy are.
   (who / get / married)

2. A: _____   B: In Washington.
   (where / they / have / the wedding)

3. A: _____   B: In six months.
   (when / it / be)

4. A: _____   B: Their friends and relatives.
   (who / they / invite)

5. A: _____   B: They're going to take a trip.
   (what / happen / after the wedding)

6. A: _____   B: To Mexico.
   (where / they / go / on their trip)

7. A: _____   B: For a week.
   (how long / they / stay / in Mexico)

8. A: _____   B: In Virginia.
   (where / Joe and Judy / live)

B Read the sentences. Write questions about the future with *Who, What, When, Where, How much,* and *How long.*

1. Bill is shopping.   _____What is he going to buy?_____
   (buy)

2. Kate is picking up her phone.   _____
   (call)

3. Mike is getting into his car.   _____
   (go)

4. The children are sleeping.   _____
   (sleep)

5. Julio is going to college now.   _____
   (graduate)

6. I'm paying for dinner.   _____
   (cost)

NAME: _____ **DATE:** _____

Review and Challenge

Find the mistake in each sentence. Circle the letter and correct the mistake.

1. **A:** I'm going to <u>Al's</u> birthday party.
                   A

   B: You <u>is going to</u> <u>have</u> a great time.
             Ⓑ   C

   Correct: _You are going to have a_ _great time._

2. **A:** Tanya <u>no is going to</u> <u>come</u> with us.
             A B   C

   B: That's too bad.

   Correct: _____

3. **A:** <u>It's</u> <u>not</u> <u>going</u> rain tomorrow.
         A B C

   B: That's good.

   Correct: _____

4. **A:** <u>Are they</u> going to <u>buy</u> a house?
            A   B

   B: No, they <u>not</u>.
                C

   Correct: _____

5. **A:** <u>Are you</u> <u>going to go</u> fishing?
          A   B

   B: Yes, I <u>do</u>.
              C

   Correct: _____

6. **A:** <u>Is</u> <u>it's</u> going to be sunny tomorrow?
        A B

   B: Yes, it <u>is</u>.
              C

   Correct: _____

7. **A:** <u>How long</u> <u>you</u> going to stay there?
           A   B

   B: <u>For</u> two weeks.
          C

   Correct: _____

8. **A:** <u>What</u> <u>it's</u> going to <u>happen</u>?
         A B   C

   B: I don't know.

   Correct: _____

9. **A:** <u>When</u> <u>is</u> dinner going to be ready?
         A   B

   B: Soon—<u>for</u> five minutes.
              C

   Correct: _____

10. **A:** <u>Who</u> <u>is it</u> going to <u>get married</u>?
          A   B   C

    B: Paul and Rosalie are.

    Correct: _____

UNIT 17 VOCABULARY EXERCISE

Complete the conversations. Use the words in the box.

got a prescription	have a pain	pharmacist	see a doctor
has the flu	~~have allergies~~	prescription	sneeze
have a cough	hurts	put on a Band-Aid	took his temperature
have a cut			

1. **Tom:** Look! I got a cat.

   Mary: Oh, no! Not a cat. I _____ have allergies _____. When I'm near a cat, I
   _____. Achooo!

2. **Jean:** What's wrong?

   Rachel: I _____ in my head. It's terrible.

   Jean: You have a bad headache. You need some medicine.

3. **Gilbert:** Where are you going?

   Mayra: To _____.

   Gilbert: What's wrong?

   Mayra: I _____. I need a _____ for some
   cough medicine.

   [Later that day]

   Gilbert: How are you feeling?

   Mayra: Pretty good. I _____ for cough medicine. The
   _____ told me to take the medicine every six hours.

4. **Mother:** Enrique is sick. I _____. It's 38.8°C (102°F).

   Father: Maybe he _____.

5. **Son:** My leg _____.

   Dad: You _____. It's not very bad. Don't move. I'm going to
   _____.

UNIT 17 GRAMMAR EXERCISES

Grammar to Communicate 1:
Should: Affirmative and Negative Statements

A   **Match the problems with the advice. Write the correct letters.**

__c__ **1.** The baby feels warm.

a. He shouldn't go to work.

_____ **2.** My teenagers are tired all the time.

b. He should put a bandage on it.

_____ **3.** Laura feels nauseous.

c. We should ~~take his temperature.~~

_____ **4.** Mark cut his hand.

d. They should sleep more.

_____ **5.** Steve has a fever.

e. You should talk to your doctor.

_____ **6.** I have a bad stomachache.

f. She shouldn't eat anything.

B   **Give advice. Write sentences with *should* or *shouldn't*.**

1. Max has a cold.   _____He should drink a lot of water._____
                                   (he / drink / a lot of water)

2. Sharon has a headache.   _____
                                   (she / take / some aspirin)

3. I think I have the flu.   _____
                                   (you / go / to work)

4. My throat is sore.   _____
                                   (you / gargle / with salt water)

5. Maybe Ellen's arm is broken.   _____
                                   (we / take / her / to the emergency room)

6. My children have earaches.   _____
                                   (they / stay / home from school)

7. The baby has a fever.   _____
                                   (we / give / her / adult aspirin)

Grammar to Communicate 2:
Should: Yes/No Questions

A   **Rewrite the questions. Use *should*. Then complete the answers.**

Is it a good idea . . .

1. . . . for sick children to go to school?

   _____Should sick children go to school?_____   No, ____they shouldn't____ .

2. . . . for people to eat fresh fruit?

   _____   Yes, _____ .

3. . . . for children to take adult aspirin?

   _____   No, _____ .

4. . . . for people to go swimming after eating?

   _____   No, _____ .

5. . . . for everyone to brush their teeth?

   _____   Yes, _____ .

6. . . . for people with the flu to exercise?

   _____   No, _____ .

B   **Ask for advice. Complete the questions with *should I*. Use the words in the box.**

drink hot tea or cold water	~~go to work or to bed~~
exercise or rest	put ice or a hot water bottle

1. _____Should I go to work or to bed_____ with a cold?

2. _____ for my sore throat?

3. _____ on my sore back?

4. _____ my tired legs?

Grammar to Communicate 3:
Should: Information Questions

A **Complete the sentences. Circle the correct answers.**

1. Who should I ask for advice?

    a. At the pharmacy.   **b.** Your doctor.

2. What should we do?

    a. Go to the emergency room.   **b.** Yes, we should.

3. What should I take for a headache?

    a. Aspirin.   **b.** Twice a day.

4. Who will fill my prescription?

    a. Your medicine.   **b.** A pharmacist.

5. How often should I take this medicine?

    a. For ten days.   **b.** Every four hours.

6.   How long should I take it?

    a. For five days.   **b.** Twice a day.

B **Write questions with *Which* and *should*.**

1. _____Which antacid should I take for my heartburn?_____
                    (antacid / I / take / for my heartburn)

2. _____
                    (cough syrup / we / buy)

3. _____
                    (doctor / he / see)

4. _____
                    (medicine / you / give / to a baby)

5. _____
                    (medicine / I / try / for my allergies)

6. _____
                    (pharmacy / we / go to)

Review and Challenge

Complete the conversation. Use the words in the box. (Be careful! There is one extra word.)

or	prescription	should	stay	temperature
pharmacy	~~see~~	shouldn't	take	times

Rosa: You look terrible. You should _____*see*_____ your doctor.
1.

Inez: I did. I saw her this morning. She gave me a _____ for some medicine.
2.

Where _____ I go to fill it?
3.

Rosa: To a _____. There's one on State Street. But you _____ go out.
4.   5.

I'll get the medicine. You should _____ home.
6.

Inez: Thanks.

Rosa: How long do you need to _____ the medicine?
7.

Inez: For ten days.

Rosa: And how often?

Inez: Three _____ a day.
8.

Rosa: Do you take it with food _____ with water?
9.

Inez: I'm not sure. Please ask the pharmacist.

UNIT 18 VOCABULARY EXERCISE

Complete the conversation. Use the words in the box.

| close to | dangerous street | high rent | low rent | pretty view | safe |
| convenient | far from | in the country | modern | public transportation | ugly |

Two college students need a place to live. They are looking in the newspaper.

Jim: Here's an apartment near the college. It has a _____ low rent _____ —just
            1.
            $450 a month.

Jorge: Where is it?

Jim: It's on College Avenue. We can walk to class. That's _____.
                                                                  2.

Jorge: I don't know. College Avenue is a _____. There are a lot of
                                              3.
            bad people on that street. It's not _____.
                                                 4.

Jim: Well, here's an apartment on Bank Street.

Jorge: Is it _____ Bus #15?
                   5.

Jim: Yes, it is. The _____ is excellent. There are lots of bus
                            6.
            stops on Bank Street.

Jorge: What's the address?

Jim: 655 Bank Street. The building is called "Student Towers."

Jorge: Oh, no! Not there! That building is _____. I
                                                 7.
            want to live in a beautiful place. And Student Towers is old. I want a
            _____ apartment.
                   8.

Jim: OK, here's an apartment on Oak Street.

Jorge: But there aren't any buses from Oak Street. It's _____
                                                             9.
            public transportation. Oak Street! That's not in the city; that's
            _____!
                   10.

Jim: I know, but it's quiet and beautiful. The apartments have a
            _____ of the streets. There's a park on Oak Street, too.
                   11.

Jorge: Great! Does the apartment have a _____, too?
                                               12.

Jim: $1,050 a month.

Jorge: That's perfect for us . . . in ten years!

UNIT 18 GRAMMAR EXERCISES

Grammar to Communicate 1:
Comparative of Adjectives

A **Read the chart. Complete the sentences. Write _A_ or _B_.**

	modern	pretty	convenient	big	expensive
Apartment A	★★★★	★	★★	★★★	★★★★
Apartment B	★	★★★	★★★★	★	★★

Chart Key:

★★★★ — ★★★ — ★★ — ★
very   not very

1. Apartment __A__ is more modern than Apartment __B__.

2. Apartment _____ is prettier than Apartment _____.

3. Apartment _____ is more convenient than Apartment _____.

4. Apartment _____ is bigger than Apartment _____.

5. Apartment _____ is more expensive than Apartment _____.

B **Complete the story. Use the comparative form of the adjectives.**

Joe and Bill are brothers. They live in small houses. Bill's house is

__smaller__ than Joe's house. Bill has only three rooms, but they are
1. (small)

_____ than the rooms in Joe's house. They are _____ and
2. (nice)   3. (clean)

_____. Bill's windows are _____. The furniture is _____,
4. (sunny)   5. (large)   6. (good)

too. Bill's house is _____ from stores than Joe's house, but it is
7. (far)

_____, and he likes that.
8. (quiet)

Grammar to Communicate 2:
Superlative of Adjectives

A   Complete the sentences. Use superlatives.

1. The living room is _____the biggest_____ room.
                              (big)

2. The kitchen is _____ room.
                          (sunny)

3. The bedroom is _____ room.
                          (quiet)

4. _____ room is the kitchen.
        (busy)

5. _____ room is the living room.
        (comfortable)

6. The bedroom is _____ room from the street.
                          (far)

B   Write sentences about Angie's apartment. Use *is* or *are* and superlatives.

1. _My apartment is the smallest apartment in the building._____
        (my apartment / small / apartment in the building)

2. _____
        (the kitchen / warm / room / in my apartment)

3. _____
        (pretty / room / my bedroom)

4. _____
        (modern / room / the new bathroom)

5. _____
        (the TV / important / thing / in the living room)

6. _____
        (the big windows / good / thing / about my apartment)

7. _____
        (my neighbors / noisy / people / in the building)

8. _____
        (the noise / bad / thing / about my apartment)

Grammar to Communicate 3:
Comparative and Superlative

A **Complete the questions. Circle the correct answers.**

1. Which country has _____ weather—England or India?

    (a. cooler)   **b.** the coolest

2. Which country has _____ cities—Venezuela, Jamaica, or Panama?

    a. bigger   **b.** the biggest

3. Which country has _____ buildings—the United States or Canada?

    a. taller   **b.** the tallest

4. Which country has _____ food—Italy, China, Thailand, or France?

    a. better   **b.** the best

5. Which country is _____ from Africa—Argentina or Australia?

    a. farther   **b.** the farthest

6. Which country is _____ for soccer—Brazil or Poland?

    a. more famous   **b.** the most famous

B **Complete the questions. Use the comparative or the superlative form. Use**
than **where necessary.**

1. What is _____the largest_____ city in your country?
                    (large)

2. Which is ____more expensive____—a beach house or a country house?
                   (expensive)

3. What is _____ place to live in your city?
                    (good)

4. What is _____ to you—a safe neighborhood or a cheap
                 (important)
    place to live?

5. Which is _____—a large, modern apartment or a small,
                   (good)
    traditional house?

6. What is _____ thing in a neighborhood—nice parks,
                 (important)
    convenient stores, good restaurants, or friendly neighbors?

7. Is a first-floor apartment _____ a sixth-floor
                                      (safe)
    apartment?

8. What is _____ thing about your neighborhood?
                  (nice)

Review and Challenge

Correct the conversation. There are seven mistakes. The first mistake is corrected for you.

Real estate agent: Welcome to Tops in Town Real Estate. How can I help you?

Client: I'm not happy with my apartment. I'm looking for a ~~biggest~~ *bigger* one, and I want to live in a more safer neighborhood.

Real estate agent: What is the more important thing to you—the apartment, the neighborhood, or the rent?

Client: All three are important! But I really want a gooder neighborhood.

Real estate agent: And how many rooms do you need?

Client: Well, I have three rooms now, and I don't want a more small apartment than that. I'm ready to pay for a most expensive place than my present apartment.

Real estate agent: OK. Well, I have three apartments in Cooper's Village. That's safest neighborhood in the city.

Client: Great. Can we go see them?

UNIT 19 VOCABULARY EXERCISE

Read about the changes. Match the changes with the statements. Write the correct letters.

__b__ **1.** Sandra got bad news.

_____ **2.** Bill and Celia are making plans.

_____ **3.** Nestor got a raise.

_____ **4.** Ed got in touch with Carmen.

_____ **5.** Tina and Rita started a business.

_____ **6.** Uriel is having a good time.

_____ **7.** The business succeeded.

a. "Your salary is now $50 more each week. Good work."

b. "I'm sorry, but the company is going to move to another city."

c. "This is a great party! Good food and good music!"

d. "Irma's Gift Store made $50,000 in the first year."

e. "Do you want to go to a concert on Saturday night?"

f. "Hi. I'm sorry I didn't call you last month. I was so busy."

g. "We opened a day-care center."

UNIT 19 GRAMMAR EXERCISES

Grammar to Communicate 1:
Will: Affirmative and Negative Statements

A Complete Rob's sentences about his future. Use *will, 'll,* or *won't.*

1. _____I'll probably finish school_____ in two years.
        (I / probably / finish / school)

2. _____ after graduation.
        (I / find / a better job)

3. _____ in the future.
        (I / not / move / to another city)

4. _____ in a few years.
        (my girlfriend and I / get married)

5. _____.
        (we / probably / not / have / a big wedding)

6. _____.
        (our families / be / happy for us)

B Rewrite the sentences about Donna's future in a new city. Use *will, 'll,* or *won't.*

1. Donna is probably going to be happy in her new city.

    Donna will probably be happy in her new city.

2. Her new job is going to be interesting.

    _____

3. She is probably going to like it.

    _____

4. She is going to find a better apartment.

    _____

5. Her rent is probably going to be higher.

    _____

6. She probably isn't going to need a car.

    _____

7. She is going to make new friends.

    _____

8. Her old friends are going to miss her.

    _____

NAME: _____ DATE: _____

Grammar to Communicate 2:
Will: Yes/No Questions

A Rewrite the questions with *will*. Then write answers.

1. Are rents going to be higher in five years?

   Will rents be higher in five years?   _Yes, they will. OR No, they won't._

2. Are computers going to be cheaper next year?

   _____   _____

3. Is there going to be a computer in every home?

   _____   _____

4. Is gas going to cost the same in three years?

   _____   _____

5. Are there going to be more bicycles on the roads?

   _____   _____

6. Are people going to drive flying cars in the year 2030?

   _____   _____

B Will things be the same next year? Write questions with *Will*.

1. Bob takes cheap vacations.   _Will Bob take cheap vacations next year?_

2. My team doesn't win a lot
   of games.   _____

3. Carl and Ann eat out every night. _____

4. Juan works ten hours a day.   _____

5. Linda doesn't have a job.   _____

6. Gas is expensive.   _____

7. Bananas are cheap.   _____

8. There aren't a lot of good
   new movies.   _____

9. I don't make a lot of money.   _____

Grammar to Communicate 3:
Will: Information Questions

A   **Match the questions with the answers. Write the correct letters.**

___c___ **1.** Who will meet someone new?   **a.** She'll be nice, pretty, and smart.

_____ **2.** What will she be like?   **b.** Soon.

_____ **3.** Where will they meet?   **c.** ~~Kenji will.~~

_____ **4.** What will they talk about?   **d.** At a party.

_____ **5.** What will happen next?   **e.** Music and school.

_____ **6.** When will they see each other? **f.** Kenji will ask for her number.

B   **Complete the conversations. Write information questions with *will*.**

1. Gary: _____When will your job end?_____
                    (when / your job / end)

   Amy: On June 30.

2. Gary: _____
                    (what / you / do / next)

   Amy: I'll look for another job.

3. Gary: _____
                    (how / you / find / another job)

   Amy: Well, first, I'll talk to a lot of people.

4. Gary: _____
                    (who / you / talk to)

   Amy: Friends, family, and co-workers.

5. Gary: _____
                    (how / they / help you)

   Amy: They'll give me ideas and suggestions.

6. Gary: _____
                    (where / your new job / be)

   Amy: Here in the city.

7. Gary: _____
                    (how often / I / see / you)

   Amy: Every weekend!

NAME: _____ DATE: _____

Review and Challenge

Find the mistake in each conversation. Circle the letter and correct the mistake.

1. **A:** The rent <u>won't probably go</u> up.
   (A)   B

   B: That <u>will be</u> good!
         C

   Correct: *The rent probably*
   won't go up.

2. **A:** <u>What will</u> the job be like?
      A

   B: <u>It's</u> will <u>probably be</u> interesting.
     B   C

   Correct: _____

3. **A:** <u>We'll</u> probably have a test <u>this Friday.</u>
      A   B

   B: That's OK. <u>It'll no</u> be hard.
               C

   Correct: _____

4. **A:** <u>Will he</u> <u>changes</u> a lot in college?
     A   B

   B: No, he <u>won't</u>.
           C

   Correct: _____

5. **A:** <u>There be</u> better cars <u>in</u> five years?
      A   B

   B: Yes, there <u>will</u>.
            C

   Correct: _____

6. **A:** <u>Will you</u> <u>be</u> home for dinner tonight?
     A   B

   B: No, <u>I'll not</u>.
         C

   Correct: _____

7. **A:** <u>What</u> <u>will it</u> happen next?
     A   B

   B: <u>They'll probably</u> change their plans.
         C

   Correct: _____

8. **A:** What <u>the weather will it</u> be like tomorrow?
             A

   B: <u>We'll</u> <u>probably have</u> a cool and sunny day.
      B   C

   Correct: _____

9. **A:** <u>When</u> <u>I will</u> find the love of my life?
      A   B

   B: I <u>don't</u> know.
       C

   Correct: _____

UNIT 20 VOCABULARY EXERCISES

Complete the conversations. Use the words in the boxes.

airplane	flight attendant	~~passengers~~	pilot	seat belt

1. **Rebecca:** Good morning, _____passengers_____. This is Flight 109 to New York. My name is Rebecca, and I will be your _____ this morning. At this time, please be sure you have your _____ on. When the _____ says it is safe, you can move around the _____.

get off	get on	subway

2. **Linda:** How do we get to the art museum on the _____?

   Rick: Well, we _____ at the Oak Park station.

   Linda: And where do we _____?

   Rick: That's easy. At the Museum station.

one-way	reserve . . . in advance	schedule	sold out
reserve	round-trip	show your ticket	train station

3. **Mr. Sato:** When do trains leave for Chicago?

   Ticket agent: Here's a train _____.

   Mr. Sato: Thanks. I want to _____ a seat to Chicago this afternoon at 1:00 P.M.

   Ticket agent: I'm sorry, but it's _____ . But there are tickets for the 5:00 P.M. train.

   Mr. Sato: OK, I'll take that.

   Ticket agent: Do you want a _____ ticket?

   Mr. Sato: No, I'm going to come back. I need a _____ ticket. I want to come back on May 3rd. Should I _____ a seat _____?

   Ticket agent: Yes, you should. Here are your tickets. Just _____ when you get on the train.

   Mr. Sato: Where do I get the train?

   Ticket agent: Track 9. It's on the other side of the _____.

UNIT 20 GRAMMAR EXERCISES

Grammar to Communicate 1:
Have to

A   **Complete the sentences with *have to* or *has to*.**

1. We _____ *have to* _____ buy the tickets for our trip today.

2. The bus driver _____ stop the bus at every bus stop.

3. Taxi drivers _____ stop at red lights.

4. I _____ go by train because I'm afraid of flying.

5. The flight attendant _____ wear a uniform.

6. All the passengers in my car _____ wear seat belts.

7. You _____ turn off your cell phone on an airplane.

8. The subway is closed. We _____ find a taxi.

B   **Read the statements. Complete the sentences with *have to* or *has to* and the words in the box.**

go to the station	pay the driver in cash	stand
open the door	reserve a seat in advance	~~wait at the bus stop~~

1. Manuel wants to take the number 4 bus. He _*has to wait at the bus stop*_ .

2. We are going to take a train to Chicago. We _____.

3. My bus is always crowded. There aren't any seats, so I _____.

4. Jim wants to fly to Orlando. He _____.

5. Leslie wants to get off the bus. The driver _____.

6. Len and Ali need to pay for their taxi ride. They _____.

Grammar to Communicate 2:
Would like

A **Rewrite the sentences. Use *would like*. Add *please*.**

1. I want to get off at this bus stop.

    _____ I would like to get off at this bus stop, please. _____

2. We want to change our seats.

    _____

3. My son wants some water.

    _____

4. My wife wants a cup of tea.

    _____

5. I want to buy a ticket.

    _____

6. We want bus schedules.

    _____

7. I want to leave on Friday.

    _____

B **Write offers with *Would you like*. Use *to* where necessary.**

1. _____ Would you like to use my phone? _____
       (use my phone)

2. _____
       (some coffee)

3. _____
       (this magazine)

4. _____
       (get off here)

5. _____
       (sit here)

6. _____
       (a window seat)

7. _____
       (a round-trip ticket)

8. _____
       (take a taxi)

Grammar to Communicate 3:
Can / Could / Would

A   Change the statements to polite requests. Use *Could I* and *please*.

I want . . .

1. . . . two tickets to Dallas.   _Could I have two tickets to Dallas, please?_

2. . . . some water.   _____

3. . . . a newspaper.   _____

4. . . . some help.   _____

5. . . . a bus schedule.   _____

6. . . . a ride to the airport.   _____

B   Write requests. Use *Can, Could,* or *Would* and the words in the box.

bring me some water	~~give me a window seat~~	look at your newspaper
~~buy a ticket for the 1:00 train~~	have a subway map	take me to the train station

1. (could) You are talking to a ticket agent at the airport.

    Could you give me a window seat?

2. (can) You are talking to a ticket agent at the train station.

    Can I buy a ticket for the 1:00 train?

3. (would) You are talking to a flight attendant on a plane.

4. (could) You are talking to another passenger on a train.

5. (would) You are talking to your taxi driver.

6. (can) You are talking to the person at the subway information desk.

NAME: _____   DATE: _____

Review and Challenge

Find the mistake in each conversation. Circle the letter and correct the mistake.

1. **A:** What <u>did</u> the flight attendant say?
             A

    B: Passengers <u>has to</u> <u>wear</u> seat belts.
               Ⓑ   C

    Correct: _Passengers have to_
                   wear seat belts.

2. **A:** <u>Can</u> I buy a ticket on the train?
           A

    B: No, you <u>have</u> reserve your seat <u>in advance.</u>
               B   C

    Correct: _____

3. **A:** Does he <u>need</u> money?
              A

    B: Yes, he <u>have to</u> pay the driver <u>in cash.</u>
               B   C

    Correct: _____

4. **A:** <u>I like</u> <u>to buy</u> a <u>round-trip</u> ticket, please.
         A   B   C

    B: That will be $80.

    Correct: _____

5. **A:** <u>We would</u> <u>like change</u> our <u>seats.</u>
           A   B   C

    B: I'm sorry, but there are no empty seats.

    Correct: _____

6. **A:** <u>Would</u> <u>you'd like</u> some coffee?
           A   B

    B: <u>No, thank you.</u>
               C

    Correct: _____

7. **A:** <u>Can</u> I help you, ma'am?
           A

    B: <u>Could you</u> <u>giving</u> me some information?
             B   C

    Correct: _____

8. **A:** <u>Would I have</u> a <u>one-way ticket</u>, please?
            A   B

    B: When <u>would you like</u> to travel?
                C

    Correct: _____

9. **A:** <u>We could</u> <u>have</u> a schedule, please?
           A   B

    B: <u>Of course.</u>
             C

    Correct: _____

Unit 1, page 1, vocabulary

A

2.	middle-aged	7.	good-looking
3.	old	8.	beautiful
4.	thin	9.	tall
5.	average weight	10.	short
6.	heavy	11.	average height

B

1. talkative   2. quiet, serious

Unit 1, page 2, grammar

Grammar to Communicate 1

A

2. am	4. is	6. am	8. are
3. is	5. am	7. are	

B

2. is, 's not   4. are, 're not   6. are, 're not
3. am, 'm not   5. are, 're not

Grammar to Communicate 2

A

2. a   3. e   4. b   5. f   6. d

B

2. Are you married? Yes, I am. OR No, I'm not.
3. Are your classmates talkative? Yes, they are. OR No, they're not.
4. Are you average height? Yes, I am. OR No, I'm not.
5. Is your best friend funny? Yes, she/he is. OR No, she's/he's not.
6. Is your teacher tall? Yes, she/he is. OR No, she's/he's not.

Grammar to Communicate 3

A

2. women	4. child	6. people, pictures
3. children	5. boys	

B

2. The men are tall.
3. The girls are smart.
4. The children are noisy.
5. The teachers are friendly.
6. The women are funny.
7. The boys are good-looking.
8. The classes are small.

Review and Challenge

Vu: Yes, ~~I am.~~ **2. I am** My name is Vu.

Yuri: Hi. I'm Yuri. This class ∧ good.   **3. is**
Vu: Is it big?
Yuri: No, ~~it~~ not. ~~Is~~ small—six ~~mans~~ and seven ~~woman~~.   **4. it's   5. It is   6. men   7. women**
Vu: Are the students nice?
Yuri: Yes, they are. The ~~studentes~~ are friendly.   **8. students**
Vu: Is ~~nice~~ the teacher ∧ ?   **9. nice**
Yuri: Yes, she is. She ~~no is~~ strict.   **10. is not**

Unit 2, page 7, vocabulary

2. niece, aunt
3. uncle, nephew
4. wife, husband
5. father, daughter
6. mother, son
7. cousins
8. brother-in-law, sister-in-law
9. grandparents
10. parents
11. grandfather
12. grandmother
13. father-in-law
14. mother-in-law

Unit 2 , page 9, grammar

Grammar to Communicate 1

A

2. my	4. Our/My	6. your
3. His	5. Their	

B

1. his parents, his grandparents
2. her cousin, her mother, her uncle
3. her brother, her son, her niece
4. their sister-in-law, their grandfather

Grammar to Communicate 2

A

2. brother's	5. children's
3. wife	6. parents'
4. Henry and June's	7. brother-in-law's

B

2. Susana's
3. Olivia and Fernando's
4. Tania's
5. Laura and Julio's OR Laura's
6. Marisol's

Answer Key

Grammar to Communicate 3

A

2. a   4. c   6. h   8. f
3. g   5. b   7. e

B

2. How old is Ned?
3. How tall is Liliana?
4. What is Polly's telephone number?
5. When is Charlie's English class?
6. Who is in the picture?
7. Where are your parents?

Review and Challenge

2. C: How old is your father's friend?
3. D: Their names are Lisa and Anita.
4. C: My cousin's husband is 6 feet 3 inches.
5. D: They're fine.
6. A: What is your aunt's telephone number?
7. B: Where is Betty and Linda's house?
8. C: When is your mother's English class?
9. C: Where is your children's school?

Unit 3, page 13, vocabulary

2. She is an attorney.
3. He is a cook.
4. She is a nurse.
5. She is a dentist.
6. He is an electrician.
7. She is an engineer.
8. He is a plumber.
9. She is a hairdresser.
10. She is an interpreter.
11. He is a mechanic.
12. He is a waiter.
13. She is a waitress.

Unit 3, page 15, grammar

Grammar to Communicate 1

A

2. a dentist   5. attorneys
3. a hairdresser   6. nurses
4. an interpreter

B

2. is a hairdresser.
3. is an interpreter.
4. is a mechanic.
5. is an engineer.
6. is a doctor.
7. are engineers.
8. are mechanics.

Grammar to Communicate 2

A

Meg is a (good) hairdresser. She is (careful). She is a (fast) worker. She isn't (messy). Meg's job is (interesting). Her boss is a (nice) woman. Meg is (happy) at her job.

B

2. a   4. b   6. a   8. b
3. b   5. b   7. a

Grammar to Communicate 3

A

2. F   3. T   4. F   5. F   6. T

B

2. a   4. the   6. a, Ø, the
3. Ø   5. the, a, Ø

Review and Challenge

2. an   6. interesting
3. mechanic   7. the
4. engineer   8. messy
5. nurses

Unit 4, page 19, vocabulary

2. shopping mall   9. office building
3. restaurant   10. café
4. hospital   11. buildings
5. airport   12. outdoor market
6. supermarket   13. stores
7. apartment building   14. hotel
8. movie theater

Unit 4, page 20, grammar

Grammar to Communicate 1

A

2. There is   4. There are   6. There are
3. There is   5. There is

B

2. is   3. are   4. aren't   5. isn't   6. is

Grammar to Communicate 2

A

2. some   4. any   6. any
3. any   5. some

B

2. are   4. is   6. aren't   8. isn't
3. aren't   5. are   7. aren't

Grammar to Communicate 3

A

1. there is
2. Are there, there aren't
3. any, a, They
4. It

B

2. Is there a river
3. Are there nice restaurants
4. Is there an old college
5. Are there good hospitals
6. Is there a lake

Review and Challenge

2. B: There is a new bank on Maple Street, too.
3. B: No, there aren't.
4. C: There are good restaurants on Water Street, too.
5. B: There are a lot of stores here.
6. C: No, there aren't any stores on Green Street.
7. C: No, there isn't.
8. A: Are there any good schools here?

Unit 5, page 24, vocabulary

A

2. bananas
3. apples
4. spinach
5. oranges
6. carrots
7. milk
8. juice
9. tea
10. soup
11. candy
12. cookies
13. eggs
14. fruit
15. vegetables
16. meat

B

2. ice cream
3. mayonnaise
4. a box of rice
5. beef
6. fish
7. chicken

Unit 5, page 26, grammar

Grammar to Communicate 1

A

2. is
3. are
4. is
5. is
6. is
7. are

B

Answers may vary.
2. is OR isn't
3. are OR aren't
4. is OR isn't
5. are OR aren't
6. is OR isn't
7. is OR isn't
8. are OR aren't

Grammar to Communicate 2

A

2. a few
3. a little
4. a little
5. a few
6. a few

B

2. a lot of
3. is
4. some
5. are
6. any
7. a little
8. a lot
9. some

Grammar to Communicate 3

A

2. Yes, there is.
3. No, there aren't.
4. Yes, there is.
5. No, there isn't.
6. Yes, there are.

B

2. How much rice is there?
3. How many cookies are there?
4. How much juice is there?
5. How many carrots are there?
6. How many eggs are there?

Review and Challenge

2. C: It's on the table.
3. A: How many potatoes are there?
4. B: How much is the candy?
5. C: There are a few bananas.
6. A: How much soda is there?
7. C: Yes, there is.
8. C: There's a little salt.
9. A: Are there any cookies in the box?

Unit 6, page 30, vocabulary

A

2. go for a walk
3. ride a bike
4. play tennis
5. play soccer
6. do exercises
7. swim

B

2. Go
3. Play
4. home
5. shower
6. Watch

Unit 6, page 32, grammar

Grammar to Communicate 1

A

2. am working / 'm working
3. are wearing / 're wearing
4. are practicing
5. is taking
6. are walking

B

3. The two women are talking.
4. They are not/aren't exercising.
5. The children are playing.
6. They are not/aren't swimming.

Answer Key

7. The man is not/isn't watching the children.
8. He is/He's sitting.

Grammar to Communicate 2

A

2. Are they swimming? Yes, they are.
3. Is he wearing a helmet? No, he's not/he isn't.
4. Is she sitting in the classroom? Yes, she is.
5. Are you learning English? Yes, I am.

B

2. Is she working, she isn't/she's not
3. Are they watching, they aren't/they're not
4. Are you talking, I am

Grammar to Communicate 3

A

2. b   3. e   4. d   5. a

B

2. What is the girl wearing?
3. Who is she talking to?
4. What is the boy doing?
5. Where is the man sitting?
6. Why is he watching TV?

Review and Challenge

2. playing   5. 'm   7. riding
3. Who   6. exercising   8. Is
4. are

Unit 7, page 36, vocabulary

2. start   6. put   10. move
3. Turn off   7. touch   11. wait for
4. Ask   8. Ask for
5. Take   9. turn on

Unit 7, page 38, grammar

Grammar to Communicate 1

A

2. Don't talk.   4. Don't sit in your room.
3. Don't take the bus.   5. Don't go to the mall.

B

2. listen   5. Take   7. open
3. Don't smoke   6. Don't be   8. Don't run
4. Eat

Grammar to Communicate 2

A

2. a   4. a   6. a
3. b   5. a   7. b

B

2. to   4. to   6. to   8. for
3. at   5. for   7. to

Grammar to Communicate 3

A

2. them   4. you   6. me
3. us   5. it   7. him

B

1. them   2. she, her   3. him, me, them, us

Review and Challenge

2. B: Wait for the bus on Main Street.
3. A: Don't smoke in the building.
4. C: Talk to Mr. Soto and ask him for help.
5. A: Don't put your clothes under your bed.
6. B: Sit down and listen to me, please.
7. C: Put the wastebasket in front of the desk.
8. A: Sit next to me and help me.

Unit 8, page 42, vocabulary

2. radio   11. CD player
3. alarm clock   12. cell phone
4. painting   13. contact lenses
5. camera   14. wallet
6. calendar   15. CDs
7. glasses   16. computer
8. records   17. credit card
9. record player   18. digital camera
10. speakers   19. DVD player
               20. DVDs

Unit 8, page 44, grammar

Grammar to Communicate 1

A

2. This is   4. That is   6. This is
3. These are   5. Those are   7. These are

B

2. This necklace is cheap.
3. These rings are nice.
4. That radio is good.
5. Those sunglasses are expensive.
6. This watch is new.
7. These earrings are pretty.

Grammar to Communicate 2

A

2. hers   4. ours   6. yours
3. his   5. theirs   7. mine

B

2. Yours   4. my   6. Her
3. Theirs   5. Ours, our   7. your

Grammar to Communicate 3

A

2. have   4. has   6. have
3. have   5. has   7. has

B

2. has a digital camera.
3. have a lot of CDs.
4. has a new radio.
5. have big TVs.
6. has two DVD players.

Review and Challenge

2. B: What's this? OR What's that?
3. B: He has a cat.
4. C: It's mine.
5. A: Those are beautiful earrings.
6. A: Dina and Rudy have a new car.
7. B: Are these your books?
8. C: We have a son, too.
9. C: They're our nephews.

Unit 9, page 48, vocabulary

2. j   4. h   6. g   8. d   10. b
3. a   5. i   7. f   9. e

Unit 9, page 49, grammar

Grammar to Communicate 1

A

2. b   5. b   8. a
3. a   6. b   9. b
4. a   7. a

B

2. eats   4. works   6. stays up
3. play   5. go

Grammar to Communicate 2

A

2. relaxes   5. likes   8. washes
3. watch   6. cries   9. has
4. eats   7. takes

B

2. My cousin fixes cars.
3. My friend has some computer games.
4. My sister studies in the evening.
5. My neighbor finishes work at 5:00.

Grammar to Communicate 3

A

2. don't stay up   4. don't watch   6. don't play
3. don't work   5. doesn't have

B

2. don't study   6. doesn't cook
3. doesn't play   7. doesn't stay up
4. doesn't watch   8. doesn't go
5. don't eat

Review and Challenge

Luisa: Hello, Slava. Is Natalya there?

Slava: No, she isn't. She ~~work~~ *1. works* from 3:00 to 11:00 on Tuesdays.

Luisa: Is she home on Wednesdays?

Slava: Well, she ~~don't~~ *2. doesn't* work, but she ~~go~~ *3. goes* to school.

Luisa: What time?

Slava: Her first class ~~start~~ *4. starts* at 9:00. She ~~isn't~~ *5. doesn't* drive—she ~~take~~ *6. takes* the bus—so she ~~leave~~ *7. leaves* at 8:10. Call her between 7:30 and 8:00.

Luisa: I ~~no~~ *8. don't* get up until 9:00 or 10:00. My classes ~~doesn't~~ *9. don't* start until 11:00.

Slava: Call her in the afternoon, then. She ~~study~~ *10. studies* at home in the afternoon.

Unit 10, page 53, vocabulary

2. sell   7. cash
3. on sale   8. receipt
4. 25 percent off   9. convenience store
5. spending money on   10. closes
6. pay for   11. opens

Unit 10, page 54, grammar

Grammar to Communicate 1

A

2. I hardly ever use cash in stores.
3. That convenience store is always open.
4. Malls are sometimes open on holidays.

Answer Key

5. We often go shopping on weekends.
6. My friends never shop at the mall.

B

3. hardly ever has good sales.
4. usually stays open late.
5. is always open on Sundays.
6. sometimes has good sales.
7. always stays open late.
8. is always open on Sundays.
9. often has good sales.

Grammar to Communicate 2

A

2. Do Bob and Mary want a new TV?, they do
3. Do I need a tie?, you don't
4. Does Anthony want a car?, he does
5. Does Maria like expensive clothes?, she does
6. Do you spend a lot on clothes?, I don't

B

3. Do you have a new computer? Yes, I do. OR No, I don't.
4. Does your friend have a new computer? Yes, he/she does. OR No, he/she doesn't.
5. Do you have an old car? Yes, I do. OR No, I don't.
6. Does your friend have an old car? Yes, he/she does. OR No, he/she doesn't.

Grammar to Communicate 3

A

2. What   4. How much
3. What kind of   5. How often

B

2. What do they sell?
3. What time does the supermarket open?
4. How often do you go shopping?
5. How much do they cost?
6. What kind of jewelry does she wear?

Review and Challenge

Karen: Do you ever shop at the Springfield Mall?

1. I often
Liz: Sure. ~~Often I~~ go there.

2. do
Karen: What time ∧ the stores open?

3. usually go
Liz: Well, I ~~go usually~~ there on Sundays, and on Sundays, they open at 10:00.

4. of
Karen: What kind ∧ things do you buy at the mall?
Liz: I like the clothes at Bettie's. I like Dave's

5. do
Sporting Goods, too. What ∧ you need at the mall?

6. have
Karen: Some new clothes. Does Bettie's ~~has~~ good prices?

7. always have
Liz: Yes. They ~~have always~~ great prices. Come with me this Sunday.

Karen: OK, thanks. What time?

Liz: How about 10:30? No, wait—make that 10:00.

8. You are never
~~Never you are~~ ready on time!

Unit 11, page 58, vocabulary

A

2. The groom is John Torres. OR John Torres is the groom.
3. The hostess is Gloria Miller. OR Gloria Miller is the hostess.
4. The host is Edward Miller. OR Edward Miller is the host.
5. It's for Elizabeth Miller.
6. No, it's an invitation for a wedding.
7. Yes, it's OK to invite a guest.

B

2. celebrate   7. dance
3. flowers   8. give me gifts
4. makes a cake   9. thank
5. have a party   10. visit
6. invite

Unit 11, page 60, grammar

Grammar to Communicate 1

A

2. to   4. for   6. for
3. for   5. to

B

2. No, but I always send my friends and family birthday cards.
3. Do you buy them flowers?
4. Sometimes I get them flowers from my garden.
5. What do you give your friends on their birthdays?
6. I like to make my friends gifts.

Grammar to Communicate 2

A

2. When do Canadians celebrate Thanksgiving?
3. Why do Americans celebrate July Fourth?

4. How do people celebrate Father's Day?
5. Where does your family celebrate New Year's Eve?
6. When do Americans celebrate Labor Day?

B

2. Where do you celebrate Mother's Day?
3. How do you celebrate Mother's Day?
4. Why do you celebrate Mother's Day?
5. When do you celebrate Father's Day?

Grammar to Communicate 3

A

2. I plan birthday parties for them.
   Who plans birthday parties for them?
3. My children make the invitations.
   Who makes the invitations?
4. Their friends bring gifts.
   Who brings gifts?
5. The children play games at their birthday parties.
   Who plays games at their birthday parties?
6. I make the birthday cake.
   Who makes the birthday cake?

B

2. A: Who do you call on their birthdays?
   B: My friends.
3. A: Who do Americans celebrate on Mother's Day?
   B: Mothers.
4. A: Who do children visit on Halloween?
   B: Their neighbors.
5. A: Who do Americans celebrate on Labor Day?
   B: Workers.
6. A: Who do people invite to holiday parties?
   B: Relatives and friends.

Review and Challenge

2. for   4. makes   6. do   8. to
3. does   5. Who   7. send

Unit 12, page 64, vocabulary

A

2. manager   5. day-care center
3. have experience 6. take care of
4. day-care worker 7. make money

B

1. real estate agent   4. am off
2. paychecks   5. make an appointment
3. co-worker

Unit 12, page 66, grammar

Grammar to Communicate 1

A

3. having, he isn't   5. work, they don't
4. eat, he does   6. working, they are

B

2. a   3. b   4. b   5. a   6. a

Grammar to Communicate 2

A

2. is working   5. understand   8. likes
3. hear   6. are doing   9. want
4. needs   7. know

B

2. They're listening to the radio now.
3. I don't like their music.
4. The boss doesn't want the radio on.
5. She's turning off the radio now.
6. My co-workers don't understand.

Grammar to Communicate 3

A

Bella: To me? Why does he want to talk to me?

Alex: He needs to ask you about the schedule.

He wants to make some changes. He likes
to talk to people first.

Bella: I like the schedule now. I don't want to change.

Alex: Talk to the boss about it. You need to go to
his office.

B

2. I need to find a job. OR I don't need to find a job.
3. I like to do office work. OR I don't like to do office work.
4. I want to learn about computers. OR I don't want to learn about computers.
5. I need to get a college degree. OR I don't need to get a college degree.
6. I like to learn new things. OR I don't like to learn new things.
7. I want to move to a different country. OR I don't want to move to a different country.

Review and Challenge

2. A: Is the manager working today?
3. C: My co-worker wants to get a new job.

Answer Key

4. A: Do you need a day off this weekend?
5. B: I am listening to the directions.
6. B: The boss understands the problems.
7. C: Do you need to make a lot of money?
8. B: What does he do in his office every day?
9. C: He doesn't want to be a real estate agent.
10. A: Does she answer the phone every day?

Unit 13, page 70, vocabulary

2. slow
3. wonderful
4. noisy
5. in a good mood
6. worried
7. clean
8. dirty
9. rude
10. angry
11. service
12. terrible
13. in a bad mood

Unit 13, page 72, grammar

Grammar to Communicate 1

A

2. were
3. were
4. were
5. was
6. was

B

2. were
3. weren't
4. was
5. were
6. were
7. was
8. was
9. wasn't

Grammar to Communicate 2

A

2. d   3. b   4. e   5. a

B

2. A: Were the stores crowded?
   B: weren't
3. A: Were there a lot of people?
   B: weren't
4. A: Were the prices good?
   B: were
5. A: Were there a lot of things on sale?
   B: were
6. A: Were the salespeople busy?
   B: weren't

Grammar to Communicate 3

A

2. When was the test?
3. Why were you home from work?
4. Where was the party?
5. How was your vacation?

B

2. Who was at the restaurant?
3. Who was Jorge with?
4. Who was on the phone a lot?
5. Who was really slow?
6. Who was Nina mad at?

Review and Challenge

Leslie: Where ~~you were~~? [2. were you]
Olga: At the beach. It was great.
Leslie: ~~Who~~ was the weather? [3. How]
Olga: It was really nice.
Leslie: ~~Was~~ you at a hotel? [4. Were]
Olga: No, ~~we~~ with Alex, at his house. [5. we were]
Leslie: Who ~~you~~ with? [6. were you]
Olga: Alex—you know, my cousin.
Leslie: Oh, yes. I remember him. ~~The house was it~~ nice? [7. Was the house]
Olga: Yes, it was, and it was only about five minutes from the beach.
Leslie: Was ~~crowded the beach~~? [8. the beach crowded]
Olga: No, ~~there~~ wasn't. There were ~~no~~ a lot of people. [9. it] [10. not]

Unit 14, page 76, vocabulary

2. forget
3. chases
4. scream
5. Take . . . back
6. catch
7. leave
8. happens
9. lose
10. change

Unit 14, page 77, grammar

Grammar to Communicate 1

A

2. called
3. invited
4. cooked
5. listened
6. arrived

B

2. I washed dishes yesterday.
3. Leo studied yesterday.
4. We waited for the bus yesterday.
5. Barbara watched the news yesterday.
6. Ari played tennis yesterday.
7. Our class started at 9:00 A.M. yesterday.
8. The bank closed at 5:00 P.M. yesterday.

Grammar to Communicate 2

A

2. ran   4. drank   6. heard   8. lost
3. forgot   5. wrote   7. knew

B

2. had   4. came   6. took
3. called   5. spent   7. did

Grammar to Communicate 3

A

2. I didn't work all night.
3. Marcia didn't wake up late.
4. We didn't make a lot of mistakes.
5. Ben didn't drink ten cups of tea.
6. Lisa didn't wash the car.
7. They didn't invite us to their wedding.
8. You didn't eat breakfast in class.

B

2. didn't play   5. didn't like
3. didn't spend   6. didn't sleep
4. didn't go out

Review and Challenge

2. went   6. came   10. talked
3. left   7. saw   11. said
4. made   8. didn't
5. was   9. talk

Unit 15, page 81, vocabulary

2. are in the military   7. graduate
3. get a driver's license   8. meet
4. retire   9. get a job
5. get married   10. become a citizen
6. have an accident

Unit 15, page 82, grammar

Grammar to Communicate 1

A

3. Did you and your class have, Yes, we did. OR No, we didn't.
4. Did you see your friends, Yes, I did. OR No, I didn't.
5. Did you and your friends do things, Yes, we did. OR No, we didn't.
6. Was it a good weekend, Yes, it was. OR No, it wasn't.

B

3. did, Yes, I did. OR No, I didn't.
4. did, Yes, I did. OR No, I didn't.

5. was, Yes, it was. OR No, it wasn't.
6. did, Yes, I did. OR No, I didn't.
7. were, Yes, they were. OR No, they weren't.
8. did, Yes, I did. OR No, I didn't.

Grammar to Communicate 2

A

2. did you work?   5. did you leave the job?
3. job did you have?   6. did you do after that?
4. did you find the job?

B

2. How old was he?
3. Where did he go to school?
4. Who took him to school every day?
5. What did he carry on his back?
6. Who was his first teacher?

Grammar to Communicate 3

A

2. for   4. for   6. ago
3. ago   5. for   7. ago

B

2. How long ago did they get married?
3. How long did they stay married?
4. How long ago did you and your wife meet?
5. How long did you stay at your first job?
6. How long ago did they build our school?

Review and Challenge

2. C: Yes, I did.
3. A: Did you live there a long time?
4. C: No, I wasn't.
5. B: What kind of movie did you see?
6. B: What happened in class yesterday?
7. B: Who gave you those flowers?
8. C: How long ago did you meet your husband?
9. B: How long did you stay at the party?
10. C: 32 years ago.

Unit 16, page 86, vocabulary

2. take   6. go on a picnic
3. stay at home   7. tonight
4. buy groceries   8. have friends over
5. pick up   9. play cards

Answer Key

Grammar to Communicate 1

A

2. are going to go
3. am going to make
4. is going to bring
5. are going to get
6. are going to play
7. are going to have

B

2. It's not going to rain/It isn't going to rain
3. It's going to be
4. It's not going to be/It isn't going to be
5. It's going to snow
6. It's not going to rain/It isn't going to rain
7. It's not going to be/It isn't going to be
8. It's not going to snow/It isn't going to snow

Grammar to Communicate 2

A

2. b   3. a   4. b   5. a   6. b

B

2. Is there going to be a party this weekend?
3. Are we going to have homework tonight?
4. Is the weather going to be nice tomorrow?
5. Are there going to be many people at the wedding?
6. Is the doctor going to call later?
7. Are you going to go to the mall soon?
8. Am I going to miss the bus?

Grammar to Communicate 3

A

2. Where are they going to have the wedding?
3. When is it going to be?
4. Who are they going to invite?
5. What is going to happen after the wedding?
6. Where are they going to go on their trip?
7. How long are they going to stay in Mexico?
8. Where are Joe and Judy going to live?

B

2. Who is she going to call?
3. Where is he going to go?
4. How long are they going to sleep?
5. When is he going to graduate?
6. How much is it going to cost?

Review and Challenge

2. A: Tanya is not going to come with us. OR Tanya isn't going to come with us.
3. C: It's not going to rain tomorrow.
4. C: No, they aren't.

5. C: Yes, I am.
6. B: Is it going to be sunny tomorrow?
7. B: How long are you going to stay there?
8. B: What is going to happen?
9. C: Soon—in five minutes.
10. B: Who is going to get married?

1. sneeze
2. have a pain
3. see a doctor, have a cough, prescription, got a prescription, pharmacist
4. took his temperature, has the flu
5. hurts, have a cut, put on a Band-Aid

Grammar to Communicate 1

A

2. d   3. f   4. b   5. a   6. e

B

2. She should take some aspirin.
3. You shouldn't go to work.
4. You should gargle with salt water.
5. We should take her to the emergency room.
6. They should stay home from school.
7. We shouldn't give her adult aspirin.

Grammar to Communicate 2

A

2. Should people eat fresh fruit?, they should
3. Should children take adult aspirin?, they shouldn't
4. Should people go swimming after eating?, they shouldn't
5. Should everyone brush their teeth?, they should
6. Should people with the flu exercise?, they shouldn't

B

2. Should I drink hot tea or cold water
3. Should I put ice or a hot water bottle
4. Should I exercise or rest

Grammar to Communicate 3

A

2. a   3. a   4. b   5. b   6. a

B

2. Which cough syrup should we buy?
3. Which doctor should he see?
4. Which medicine should you give to a baby?

5. Which medicine should I try for my allergies?
6. Which pharmacy should we go to?

Review and Challenge

2. prescription	5. shouldn't	8. times
3. should	6. stay	9. or
4. pharmacy	7. take	

Unit 18, page 96, vocabulary

2. convenient	8. modern
3. dangerous street	9. far from
4. safe	10. in the country
5. close to	11. pretty view
6. public transportation	12. high rent
7. ugly	

Unit 18, page 97, grammar

Grammar to Communicate 1

A

2. B, A   3. B, A   4. A, B   5. A, B

B

2. nicer	5. larger	7. farther
3. cleaner	6. better	8. quieter
4. sunnier		

Grammar to Communicate 2

A

2. the sunniest	5. The most comfortable
3. the quietest	6. the farthest
4. The busiest	

B

2. The kitchen is the warmest room in my apartment.
3. The prettiest room is my bedroom.
4. The most modern room is the new bathroom.
5. The TV is the most important thing in the living room.
6. The big windows are the best thing about my apartment.
7. My neighbors are the noisiest people in the building.
8. The noise is the worst thing about my apartment.

Grammar to Communicate 3

A

2. b   3. a   4. b   5. a   6. a

B

3. the best	6. the most important
4. more important	7. safer than
5. better	8. the nicest

Review and Challenge

Client:	I'm not happy with my apartment.
	1. bigger I'm looking for a ~~biggest~~ one, and I
	2. want to live in a ~~more~~ safer neighborhood.
Real estate agent:	*3. most* What is the ~~more~~ important thing to you—the apartment, the neighborhood, or the rent?
Client:	All three are important! But I really
	4. better want a ~~gooder~~ neighborhood.
Real estate agent:	And how many rooms do you need?
Client:	Well, I have three rooms now, and I
	5. smaller don't want a ~~more small~~ apartment than that. I'm ready to pay for a
	6. more ~~most~~ expensive place than my present apartment.
Real estate agent:	OK. Well, I have three apartments
	7. the in Cooper's Village. That's ∧ safest neighborhood in the city.
Client:	Great. Can we go see them?

Unit 19, page 101, vocabulary

2. e	4. f	6. c
3. a	5. g	7. d

Unit 19, page 102, grammar

Grammar to Communicate 1

A

2. I'll find a better job/I will find a better job
3. I won't move to another city
4. My girlfriend and I will get married
5. We probably won't have a big wedding
6. Our families will be happy for us

B

2. Her new job will be interesting.
3. She'll probably like it. OR She will probably like it.
4. She'll find a better apartment. OR She will find a better apartment.
5. Her rent will probably be higher.
6. She probably won't need a car.
7. She'll make new friends. OR She will make new friends.
8. Her old friends will miss her.

Answer Key

Grammar to Communicate 2

A

2. Will computers be cheaper next year?, Yes, they will. OR No, they won't.
3. Will there be a computer in every home?, Yes, there will. OR No, there won't.
4. Will gas cost the same in three years?, Yes, it will. OR No, it won't.
5. Will there be more bicycles on the roads?, Yes, there will. OR No, there won't.
6. Will people drive flying cars in the year 2030?, Yes, we will. OR No, we won't. OR Yes, they will. OR No, they won't.

B

2. Will my team win a lot of games next year?
3. Will Carl and Ann eat out every night next year?
4. Will Juan work ten hours a day next year?
5. Will Linda have a job next year?
6. Will gas be expensive next year?
7. Will bananas be cheap next year?
8. Will there be a lot of good movies next year?
9. Will I make a lot of money next year?

Grammar to Communicate 3

A

2. a   3. d   4. e   5. f   6. b

B

2. What will you do next?
3. How will you find another job?
4. Who will you talk to?
5. How will they help you?
6. Where will your new job be?
7. How often will I see you?

Review and Challenge

2. B: It will probably be interesting.
3. C: It won't be hard.
4. B: Will he change a lot in college?
5. A: Will there be better cars in five years?
6. C: No, I won't.
7. B: What will happen next?
8. A: What will the weather be like tomorrow?
9. B: When will I find the love of my life?

Unit 20, page 106, vocabulary

1. flight attendant, seat belt, pilot, airplane
2. subway, get on, get off
3. schedule, reserve, sold out, one-way, round-trip, reserve . . . in advance, show your ticket, train station

Unit 20, page 107, grammar

Grammar to Communicate 1

A

2. has to   5. has to   7. have to
3. have to   6. have to   8. have to
4. have to

B

2. have to go to the station
3. have to stand
4. has to reserve a seat in advance
5. has to open the door
6. have to pay the driver in cash

Grammar to Communicate 2

A

2. We would like to change our seats, please.
3. My son would like some water, please.
4. My wife would like a cup of tea, please.
5. I would like to buy a ticket, please.
6. We would like bus schedules, please.
7. I would like to leave on Friday, please.

B

2. Would you like some coffee?
3. Would you like this magazine?
4. Would you like to get off here?
5. Would you like to sit here?
6. Would you like a window seat?
7. Would you like a round-trip ticket?
8. Would you like to take a taxi?

Grammar to Communicate 3

A

2. Could I have some water, please?
3. Could I have a newspaper, please?
4. Could I have some help, please?
5. Could I have a bus schedule, please?
6. Could I have a ride to the airport, please?

B

3. Can/Could/Would you (please) bring me some water(, please)?
4. Can/Could I (please) look at your newspaper (, please)?
5. Can/Could/Would you (please) take me to the train station(, please)?
6. Can/Could I (please) have a subway map(, please)?

Review and Challenge

2. B: No, you have to reserve your seat in advance.
3. B: Yes, he has to pay the driver in cash.
4. A: I'd like/I would like to buy a round-trip ticket, please.
5. B: We would like to change our seats.
6. B: Would you like some coffee?
7. C: Could you give me some information?
8. A: Could I have/Can I have a one-way ticket, please?
9. A: Could we have a schedule, please?